Forty-Eight Years in the Trenches

The accounts of a teacher in the City of New York

by Ira Zornberg

Forty-Eight Years in the Trenches

The accounts of a teacher in the City of New York

by Ira Zornberg

This book is dedicated to my wife,
Judith Zornberg, and our children,
who have lived with my constant
assertion regarding the value of
studying history in order to make
this world a better place.

I also dedicate this book to all
teachers who take pride in improving
our craft and demonstrate concern
for the well being of our students.

TABLE OF CONTENTS

Introduction

Teaching is a wonderful profession. It offers the teacher an opportunity to change the world for the better. Teaching a good lesson is like taking the stage in a theatrical performance. Listening to students debate and draw conclusions at the end of a lesson, which is evidence of learning, is like the applause of an appreciative audience. Each lesson offers an opportunity to introduce skills, ideas and moral values. Having that opportunity is a gift.

Encouraged by my dad, who loved history, political science and philosophy, and who recognized that I shared his love of those subjects, I became a history teacher. It was a profession in which I found real joy. I became a social studies teacher in the New York City public schools in 1961. In 1986, I became an assistant principal in charge of social studies, first at Thomas Jefferson H.S, and then served at George Westinghouse Vocational and Technical High School in Brooklyn. During the last ten years of my career, I served as assistant principal in charge of social studies at New Dorp High School on Staten Island. The schools in which I served, located in very different neighborhoods were dramatically different from each other, and my accounts of each will make the reader aware of the great diversity in this city. At no time did I stop being a teacher. As assistant principal in charge of social studies, I taught two classes each term in addition to working with the teachers of my departments to improve the quality of instruction. As my story unfolds, I will tell you how I came to serve in as many schools as I did and what I learned in each.

I am writing this account of my years in that system for many reasons. I believe in the importance of history, and I would like my readers to have a truthful insight into what took place in the world of education in New York City over the past 48 years. It should give the reader perspective, a precondition for change. This book is both biographical and critical. It is personal account, but in seeking a wider audience, it is my hope that the reader will recognize the good that is possible and the steps required to achieve it.

Many of the best known accounts of New York City's public schools, published to the acclaim of the mass media, were written by people who taught for only a few years and quit, because of what they called "personal frustration." Their accounts provided sound bites and headlines which made them popular. This account is written by someone who often addressed worst case scenarios over the long term and took steps to address them.

At the conclusion of this book, I will make a few recommendations. However, it is my hope that long before that point you will have drawn many of your own conclusions as to what positive steps need to be taken to improve the system as you share my experiences during my "Forty-Eight Years in the Trenches."

Chapter I – The child of immigrants

I am the child of immigrants. Both of my parents came from what was the Austrian-Hungarian Empire and became part of Poland after World War I. My mother's family had its savior, uncle Jake Green, who brought the family to America shortly after World War I. My father had an uncle, Eli Zornberg who sponsored my dad in 1928. My mother, Marion Scher was a very bright and energetic woman who had a limited formal education. She came to the United States at about the age of ten, completed the eighth grade in a public school and briefly went to evening continuation school. My mother's sister, Ruth, who was younger, completed high school. My mother recounted with joy how she was loved in elementary school by her teachers, for whom she made coffee. She worked from about the age of fifteen in a nearby chemical company.

Being the eldest daughter in a traditional, religious Jewish home, she assumed the responsibility of caring for her parents, her older brother Hymie, and younger sister, Ruth. That was to continue throughout their adult lives. My grandmother, Sarah, who had borne ten children, only of which three survived, suffered from asthma, something she probably developed from plucking chickens in my grandfather's small kosher butcher store in the Brownsville section of Brooklyn. After the death of my grandfather, my grandmother came to live with us. Tragically, this very good lady lapsed into senility, which as painful as it was to my mother, led to her being placed in a nursing home. To feed her daily, my mother became a sales lady in Mayrock's, what was then a very fine, up-scale home furnishing store located only a few blocks from the nursing home. My mother would go from Mayrock's to feed her mother each day until her passing. In later years, after my

6

parents moved from Eastern Parkway to Brighton Beach, my mother sold dresses, worked in a health food store, and completed her working years, as she would boast, by making overstuffed sandwiches for students at Grady Vocational High School in Brooklyn. She was a strong woman who demonstrated the belief that you could do anything well if you were determined to do so. She was very a protective mother, a wonderful cook, and a very proud, devoted wife.

My mother was incredibly proud to have been married to my dad, Emanuel Zornberg, an exceptionally bright, highly self-educated man. By trade, my dad was a furrier, a blue collar worker. It was a trade to which he had been introduced by the uncle who had paid for his steamship ticket in steerage to America. In the years immediately following World War I, a sentiment developed that the U.S. should avoid any further European involvement. The other side of the coin was that immigration to the U.S. was limited. With a fixed number established, preference was given to immigrants from northern and western Europe (those with Anglo-Saxon genetic traits), and fewer admissions from southern and Eastern Europe. Given the restrictive immigration quotas for Eastern Europe (my dad now lived in Poland, a nation recreated out of the Austrian and Russian Empires after World War I), he was fortunate to have been admitted to the United States in 1928. My father came to America when he was already twenty-eight years of age. He came to earn enough money to sustain his family in Europe, his father having suffered a stroke. He hoped to be able to bring his family to America. He had an intuition that he would never see his father again and he was correct. After the death of his father, he prevailed upon a relative in

Canada, which had its own restrictive quotas to sponsor his sister, Sophie, as a maid. She, in turn, brought over her mother - Rivka, her brother -Mayer, and her sister -Rae. My dad's oldest and perhaps most beloved sister, Raisa and her husband and three children were murdered by the Nazis in their hometown, Chorostkov, in September 1943. Shortly after World War II, a distant cousin who had survived stayed with us for a while and recounted how he had hidden in an attic and seen Raisa and her family driven into a gas van on Rosh Hashanah, 1943. I do not recall one mention of this subject by my dad in our home while I was growing up. On one occasion, my mother confided that my dad often had nightmares about the death of his sister.

Being a worker in a seasonal trade, my dad was unemployed for about four months every year. I was always conscious of the times when my family seemed to be scratching bottom. To survive, my dad, an excellent designer, began a small fur remodeling business in the house. My mother, a very good looking woman, was his model. Showing off her Persian coat and beautifully made jackets, she drummed up business in the neighborhood. This small business, making and repairing fur coats in one room of our apartment allowed us to muddle through.

My dad, a worker in a fur shop in Manhattan would always go to work with a shirt and tie, shed them at work (where he nailed and made coats out of skins) and return home clad as a gentleman. He was an intellectual. He had reached the age of 13 working in an uncle's mill in the town of Chorostkov (a town to which his mother and her six children fled during a bombardment of their nearby town of Usiatin) during World War I. His father, who had been in the Austrian Hungarian Home Guard, was called up and fought in the Army for four years. I am uncertain as to how he did it, but in the years following the war, my father had virtually educated himself. He could read and write English before he came to America. He could speak, read and write German, Polish, Ukrainian, Yiddish, Hebrew, and English. With a beautiful handwriting, he wrote letters in English to relatives in America for his townspeople. He could recite the poems of Heine, Goethe and Schiller in German verbatim, and he had a deep love of history. Having been born into a family that had once been Chasidic, he had somehow been affected by the war and post war years in a way that made him less religious. He had belonged to a Zionist youth group and had once dreamed of immigrating to Palestine, but family needs made America his choice. During the depression years, shortly after he married my mother, he purchased a set of Encyclopedia Britannica and paid it out. The most prized piece of furniture in our home was a secretary, which had book shelves above and drawers, one of which opened up into a desk top in the middle. His book shelves were filled with books of poetry, philosophy and history. Many of those volumes were devoted to Jewish history. My dad signed his own name into each volume obtained. He loved books. In my desire to be close to him, I read most of the history books in his library as soon as I was able to. It was my father who saw my love of history and who encouraged me to go to college and major in history. Almost all the kids on my block were the children of garment workers or hat makers, but only few went to college. While working full time at Par Motor Parts after graduating from Thomas Jefferson High School, it was because of his encouragement that I went to Brooklyn College at night.

There are certain things I remember about my dad to this day. As a child of no more than four years old, during World War II, I recall his taking me to Lincoln Terrace Park in a stroller. Suddenly, when hearing an airplane over head, he tossed me to the ground and covered me with his body. As a teenager, after coming home from a hard day's labor, he would take me to the park, tie off two ends of a net and play badminton. When I signed up for Brooklyn College and went to take a swimming test which was seemingly required, he accompanied me. Looking for me when I did not come out quick enough, he stumbled into the women's lockers before he found me. Later in life, he wrote a biographical account of his life from the start of World I until he came to America. He had an excellent handwriting and an excellent mastery of the English language. His example may be one of the reasons that I am writing this book. Recalling the role models of my parents,

13

is a reminder of the importance of one's family in being moved to achieve. The foundation for personal achievement begins at home. A good question for educators is not whether, but how to engage parents so that they will motivate their children to achieve. At a time when there are so many divorces, single parents and new family configurations, intelligent planning is required. Every school must try to make the school the center of communal life, in its own way. Had it been possible for me to have later been selected as principal of Thomas Jefferson High School, a school located in a very economically depressed area, I would have spent money on evening and weekend programs training parents and adults in the use of technology, and in developing a system of job placement. Schools, especially in economically depressed areas, need to become centers of communal life. Educational leaders in each school must devise programs consistent with the needs

of their own communities.

Chapter II – Memories Are Forever

Even good teachers fail to realize that how they teach and relate to students will impact the lives of their students long afterwards. To this very day, I recall the teachers who had the greatest impact upon me in both positive and negative ways, and whose conduct would influence how I would behave as a teacher.

My high school grades in math were rarely more than in the 70's. As a result, I was never programmed for an honor's class in history or Spanish, subjects in which I excelled, nor do I ever recall being encouraged by a guidance counselor to take more challenging courses in subjects in which I did excel. I received a very different education from my future wife. In her education at Lafayette   High   School,   she   was   in   a honor's program. She was programmed for electives in English literature, and she learned how to write term papers, long before I learned to do so in college. She was taken to plays in Manhattan theatres and required reading was the *New York Times* Sunday Reviews. Being in an honor's French class, she was given high grades, almost automatically without ever really being able to speak the language. Later as a teacher, I was asked if I would accept students who had been programmed in the general track into my academic track American History classes when a programming problem arose. Some teachers made a big deal out of accepting students from a lower track and viewed what I was doing as involving some great sacrifice. I accepted students from the general track into my academic classes and some were exceptional. Getting kids to perform maximally and creative programming should be among the responsibilities of all guidance counselors, especially at the high school level.

My memories about my teachers are mixed. Upon entering Thomas Jefferson High School in Brooklyn, I found myself in Mr. Rosenman's geometry's class. I can't recall his ever asking me or any other student whether we were having difficulty or needed assistance. I do not recall any concrete examples being given of how geometry would be of value to people in everyday life. I had grades in the low 60's and he failed me. As fate would have it, I found myself repeating Geometry I in his class in the spring term. It was the only course in high school I ever failed. One day during this second term, we met in the student cafeteria. He stopped me and said, " Zornberg, what do you think you deserve?" I was taken aback. In his class, the second time around, I was running an average in the 80's. Without much thought, I unfortunately replied "I would be happy to pass." He gave me a 65%. In those days, it was unusual for one to complain, so 65% became part of my overall average. The only value of this experience, is in remembering how it hurt. I pledged mentally that I would never be as cavalier as he was with me, nor would I accept that mode of conduct on the part of teachers in my department when I later became a supervisor.

I had Geometry II with a wonderful lady, Bea Lowe, who was a home economics teacher. Probably short of a class in her discipline, she was asked to teach one section of geometry. I got a grade in the 80's on the Geometry Regents. I did well because of how she taught. Vocational subject teachers are often looked down upon by "academics." The reality is that they are often the most effective teachers. They require students to read directions carefully, ask students to explain what they have read, and then direct students to complete a product. As opposed to theoretical academics in which it is most often difficult to be certain that a student has learned, students in vocational educational classes must produce a product, and in doing so one can see whether learning has taken place. Lowe made education meaningful to me by explaining the importance of the subject in planning and design, employing the same methods of teaching her students how to prepare a dish. Most important, she was a lively and caring person. To remember this five-foot little lady, 50 + years later is indicative of how important success in her class was to me.

Noting my grades in math, my American History teacher, who also doubled as a part time grade advisor and guidance counselor, took it upon himself to advise my mother on open school night that I was not   college material. One must remember that my mother had been an immigrant child with a limited formal education. She clearly looked up to teachers as people of importance. Fortunately, she was also a tough lady who did not believe everything anyone told her. She told me what he said without making an issue of it. Over the years, I have witnessed many guidance counselors whose motivation in becoming counselors was that they would escape the classroom, lesson planning and serious teaching. Not only did this part time teacher / counselor render this judgment, but since I was in his history class, running an average well in the 90's, he lowered my grade to an 85% and refused to exempt me from the final. I believe he rationalized what he did by telling himself, "he had high standards." To him, a student who did not do well in math could not possibly be one of the top students in his class. He was wrong.

Very different were Messrs. Pinelis and Shupack, two teachers who served as models for me. Mr. Dave Pinelis was my World History teacher. He saw how engaged I was in discussing contemporary issues, in those days (issues in the late 1950's related mostly to the "cold war") and he selected me for a special activity. Each term, a small number of students were given recognition in his classes by being able to pose questions to their fellow students about the subject then being studied. He made us take on the roles of a teacher. I remember wearing a sports jacket to class and formulating and asking a question about the effects of World War I. It was amazing. I remember him fondly. When I would later write a short book entitled, *"How to be an effective social studies teacher,"* I named him as one of the people to whom it was dedicated.

In my senior year, I worked in the Square Deal drug store on Stone Avenue in the Brownsville section of Brooklyn. I delivered medicines in the low income housing projects and cleaned shelves. I felt honored to be of help to adults by delivering prescriptions to people who seemed frail. I felt I was doing something important and was deeply appreciative when these people, who lived in a low income housing project, gave me a tip, usually a quarter. I was convinced that most of them could barely afford it. Cleaning the shelves awakened my childhood asthma (which I had begun to outgrow). I lost more than a month of school. At this time, in my senior year, I was taking Earth Science I and II; Mr. Shupak was my teacher. Many other teachers, including my homeroom teacher, seemed unwilling to believe how sick I was. When I returned to school, Shupak gave me reading materials for both courses. I got in the high 80's on the Earth Science   Regents

Examination, and he gave me a similar final grade in both courses. He was a really good person. In my memories and years of teaching, Pinelis and Shupak served as my models. Years later, I would give students who missed work at school work to complete at home. It really makes little difference as long as one masters the material. While at home for a month, I got up each morning and completed a chapter in each required subject. I taught myself enough Trigonometry, so as to be able to pass that class when I returned to school. I remember shocking the teacher when I got 57 points out of 60 on the first part of his midterm examination. It was part of my process of growing up and of self-realization; I suddenly felt aware that I was changing. I was about sixteen or seventeen. I felt proud of myself. The encouragement of some very fine teachers was important in helping me to see myself as capable of achievement.

Despite my 79.9 overall average, and having failed Geometry I, I graduated from Thomas Jefferson six months early because I had completed essential course work in summer school. With a grade of 79.9, however, I was not automatically accepted to Brooklyn College on the basis of my grades. I therefore took an entrance examination, which was another way to win admission. The admission score required was 154; I scored 153.5 and I was rejected. They took their cut off point seriously. Encouraged by my dad, I went to Brooklyn College at night. I had to pay for my courses (day school was free), but I was fortunate that it was only $20 a credit. In one year, while working full time at Par Motor Parts, I took 15 credits and emerged with a 3.5 (B plus/A-) average. Having an average over a B, I was admitted to day school, which was free, the following September (1958). I had loved going to college at night. Here I was, a 17 year old kid, interpreting events in world history with mature adults and being addressed by my professors as Mr. Zornberg. I loved going home at night and reading historical documents which were part of the global history curriculum required for all students. I read them with almost religious devotion. I found joy in learning about things of which I had never known. I completed two history courses, an economics course and two Hebrew courses. Getting into day school was a gift from heaven. The people whose idea it was to admit those who achieved in evening school deserve to be honored. Had the cost been out of reach, neither my wife nor I would have been able to go to college.

With the exception of minimum registration and lab fees and books (probably less than $50) Brooklyn College was free. While maintaining realistic standards for admission, it is my feeling that all students who are willing to work hard and perform well should be able to obtain a nearly free education. The thought of being poor never occurred to me. I lived in a four floor walk up apartment, where the superintendent was directed to shut down the heat as soon as it provided the slightest amount of heat to tenants on the top floor. I knew the strains of my dad's seasonal unemployment, but poor, I never thought about it.

At Brooklyn College, I studied Hebrew, and for the first time began to understand what I was reading in the Bible. I found my heroes among the prophets who insisted upon proper human behavior towards others. Wanting to be like my father, I also taught myself to read the Yiddish papers. For my Master's degree requirement, I took an additional Spanish course and passed the language examination. Having anticipated continuing for a PHD, I also took German. I was complimented for my excellent pronunciation in German, but I found that taking the language, in which my father could recite poems, was difficult emotionally. I was aware that my aunt, her husband, and three children were murdered by the Nazis only 19 years earlier. I was asked by the language department to major in languages, but I chose to stay with history. I took more than 12 undergraduate history courses (36 credits), and an equal number as part of the Master's program. I loved my subject.

The Master's program at Brooklyn College was amazing. I took six credits during each summer session, and other courses in the evenings. Some the teachers of each course were visiting professors from prestigious universities and were some of the most prominent scholars in their fields. I remember Professor Pessen, a scholar, who taught at Columbia University, and who wrote extensively about Jacksonian democracy. One of the unresolved debates in his class was whether Andrew Jackson really believed in democracy (the voice of the common man) or whether he was an authoritarian personality who embraced the causes of the "common man" so that they would favor him.

Another brilliant professor was Professor Hyman from Stanford University in California. He taught an excellent course about the Civil War and Reconstruction. I recall the debate over whether Congressional Reconstruction after the Civil War was a logical necessity or whether it had been too hard on the south and responsible for a terrible white backlash. Studying history raises questions not only about the past; it provides perspectives for societal developments in our own time.

I wrote my master's thesis about *Leisler's Rebellion.* It was entitled, "Jacob Leisler: Defender of the Colony of New York." Anyone interested can find it on microfilm in the Brooklyn College library. Leisler, an immigrant from Germany, a former soldier, who settled in colonial New York, was entrusted with the defense of the colony shortly after the start of the "Glorious Revolution" in England. James II, his Catholic wife and newborn son were ousted by parliament. Though it was at first bloodless, it was to have military implications. In exile in France, James raised an army and invaded Ireland. In America, the Dominion of New England (joining of New York with the New England colonies under James II) had been overthrown by resentful Puritans in Massachusetts. In New York there was fear of an invasion from Canada. Leisler, a former soldier, was entrusted with leadership by merchants and farmers. Leisler organized the first inter-colonial expedition against Quebec. The aristocratic Philipses, Van Courtands and Bayards, who hated Leisler, convinced a newly arrived Governor to arrest Leisler, find him guilty of treason and carry out his execution without sending him back to England. Politics in New York would long see Leislerians in conflict with anti-Leislerians. Politics can be deadly and this has not changed.

My mentor in completing my master's thesis was Professor Robert East. East was a wonderful soft spoken man, a scholar of American Colonial History and a mid-westerner. He was a published author of many books about the American Revolution. He advised me and told me to rewrite parts of my thesis. I did so and received departmental approval of my Master's thesis in History. Having read some of the best books on each subject in

American History, and being able to recall their themes and supporting arguments, I was ready for bear.

In every institution, there are wonderful people and people who are not so wonderful at all. Among the nicest people I had at Brooklyn College was Raymond DeRoover, a professor from Belgium whose scholarship focused on the Medici and their banking practices during the Renaissance. In his class, I learned how medieval bankers gave loans in one currency and avoided usury laws (The Catholic Church did not allow interest on loans) by collecting the same amount in currencies with greater value. In a course on the Renaissance, he made one feel as if I was present in Florence in the days of Lorenzo di Medici.

The low point in my Brooklyn College experience was my experience with Professor Jesse Clarkson, the so-called "Russian expert." I took a course with him about political systems of Europe. When he lectured about the Weimar Republic which preceded the Nazis coming to power and then about post war Germany, I raised my hand and asked why there was no mention of the Nazis and their murder of the Jews in Europe. His face turned red, and he began to shout about how the Jews always thought about gentiles having "goyishe kep", non-Jewish heads, implying that Jews considered non-Jews inferior. He was justifying his omission because of a feeling he had about them that was deeply rooted in his mind. He was teaching a class filled which Jewish young people and emotionally hated Jews in the abstract. I do not remember every word in his anti-Semitic rant, but it was the first time that I had ever encountered anything like this. What I find even more upsetting, in retrospect, was the deafening silence in the classroom at that time. No one said a word.

Another horror story at Brooklyn College involved Professor Cummings, acting chairman of the history department in the early 1960's. One of the requirements for a master's degree program in history at Brooklyn College was that one pass a written examination in history (in addition to the language and thesis requirements). There were five essays on the written examination. I knew the historiography (interpretations of different historians in almost every field) and I answered them with confidence. I received a letter indicating that I had failed. I went to see Cummings. This was shortly after the assassination of President Kennedy. Cummings stated that my failure was due to my "liberal opinions." What was my liberal opinion? It was that Andrew Jackson had increased the powers of the president rather than limited them. It reminds me how in more recent times we hear "conservative" commentators denouncing Republican President Theodore Roosevelt as a statist, whatever that means.

We were alone in his office. He began to chuckle that the Kennedy assassination would bring an end to rule by the Kennedy clan. In the book *"The Sunflower"* by Simon Wiesenthal, he tells an interesting story. He reveals that he as an inmate in a Nazi concentration was once taken to the bed of a dying SS man who told how he had carried out mass murder and then on the verge of his own death asked "forgiveness from a Jew." Wiesenthal recounted that unable to respond he had simply left the room. This is what I did while Cummings chuckled. I did not know how to respond. The next time I took the exam, it was evaluated by a new chairperson, a woman in whose class I had once studied ancient history and I passed.

My most lasting accomplishment at Brooklyn College was my dating Judith Margolis, whom I married when she was 19 and I was 22 in 1962. I graduated from Brooklyn College in June 1961, and I began looking for my first regular teaching position.

Chapter III – Taking the field

Moving from school to school was part of both my early and later teaching experiences. My first regular teaching position was at Eastern District High School in the Williamsburg section of Brooklyn. In the early 1960's, probably as a result of the baby boom, there were many openings for new teachers. I had a license as a regular substitute teacher in social studies, and I began to call around to the high schools. When I called Eastern District, Mrs. Francis Lief asked me to come in for an interview. Lief was a tall woman with a full head of gray hair. I told her the courses I had taken in undergraduate school (I had only begun my Master's courses), and she offered me a position. There were many older teachers, and she had also hired a number of other young men and women. I was not aware of it at the time, but Lief must have been one of the very few female assistant principals in social studies in the city of New York. I will always owe her my appreciation for that opportunity. I loved my first job. I got up each morning, dressed in my mohair suit, white shirt and tie, borrowed my dad's car and drove down Bedford Avenue into Williamsburg. I was twenty years old.

The Old Eastern District High School, a large stone building, was located in what was then a very ethnically mixed neighborhood. The Williamsburg Bridge had been completed in 1903 and it connected the lower east side of Manhattan's Delancey Street with the northern tier of Brooklyn. The lower east side had been one of the most populated immigrant neighborhoods. Most of its inhabitants at the turn of the century were eastern European Jews and Italians. It was one of the neighborhoods about which crime reporter Jacob Riis wrote in his book *How the*

Other Half Lives and *Battle with the Slum*. Riis defined a slum as an area containing "people left behind." He described six floor tenements with outhouses, overcrowding, violence and depression. He agonized over the spread of the slum. With the opening of the Williamsburg Bridge many found their way to Brooklyn. Williamsburg contained the Brooklyn Navy yard, which built vessels for the Union navy during the civil war (*The Brooklyn* was one of the vessels sent by Lincoln to Fort Sumter in 1861), and was very productive in building many of the vessels for the American navy during World War II. After World War II, many Chassidic Jews (ultra orthodox Jews) who survived the Nazis, led by their rabbis (whom their followers looked upon as God's representatives on Earth) began to settle in Williamsburg. The children of the Chassidic Jews did not attend the public schools, but most other Jewish children did. Eastern District High School contained children of every race and religion, probably the children of blue collar workers who had worked in the Brooklyn Navy Yard during World War II. The majority were Jewish and Italian, but I also remember Polish, black and Hispanic kids. They all acted and spoke to each other in the same way. It was a natural mix. Race was never an issue. In that way, it was clearly a good time. I assigned homework and students did it. I remember teaching both World and American History. Classes were assigned, but Lief was not a teacher trainer. On one occasion, I remember her asking me to sit in on her class, but there was no discussion afterwards. I did not know what I was supposed to have seen.

In the fall of 1961, during the end of my first term as a teacher, Mrs. Lief informed me that I would be teaching the Regents Preparation class in American History which would meet an hour before regular classes began. I was not asked, I was told. Regents examinations, statewide examinations in each subject, were at that time far more difficult than they are today. Passing those examinations in New York was the key to a Regents diploma, a prerequisite for college admission. They required students to demonstrate a significant knowledge of content; today's exams focus more on reading interpretation and demonstrating minimum competency writing skills.

Regents Preparation began at about 7:15 A.M. and it was a class for which there was no remuneration for the teacher. This class was given to me in addition to my regular five classes. I got to teach this class not because of my proven skills, but because I had the least seniority. Preparing for the class, beginning instruction an hour earlier and teaching without pay was not something that most teachers were interested in doing. I felt honored to have had the opportunity to stand in front of this class and methodically share what I knew. The coursework I had taken prepared me to explain, each morning, in chronological order the issues of each period in American History, and approaches of different presidents in addressing them. I enjoyed it. I prepared carefully, covered every important development in U.S. history of which I was aware and the class was packed every day. I like to think that the class was packed because I was good; I believe that I was, but it may also have been because I was young and in today's lingo, the kids might have considered me "cool." I was 21 years old.

At the end of the first term in February 1961, I was called in to Mrs. Lief's office and told that the principal, Mr. Michaelson wanted me to accompany a senior trip to

Washington D.C. during the Passover/Easter break. I knew I had little choice. When the holidays approached, I packed a bag with a few Matzos (I came from a home in which we did not eat leavened bread during Passover) and I was off. In retrospect, it was wonderful. Of course, there was no remuneration for being a chaperone, but I had my own hotel room. I had once stayed in a hotel in the Catskill Mountains, but never before in a Washington, D.C. hotel that was luxurious. I had never visited the nation's capital and visiting the Washington Monument, Jefferson and Lincoln Memorials and Congress was amazing. I had always thought of a full room when thinking of Congress. Now, in visiting the House of Representatives, I saw one speaker chairing the House while another was speaking to a virtually empty chamber. Every word of his, however, would be included in the Congressional Record. He was setting a stage, for he certainly would be telling his constituents back home of his struggle on behalf of their cause.

One night around midnight, a young lady came knocking at my door in her pajamas and bath robe. She said that she wanted to share a piece of my matzos. She was a beautiful Italian girl. We spoke briefly and I said good night. I was "square" and I don't regret it. The memory, however, is exciting after all these years.

Teaching is a learning experience. I recall teaching a Global 4 class which covered World Wars I and II. I found *The Black Book* in my father's library. It was printed no more than two years after the end of World War II and described the systematic steps taken by the Nazis to exterminate the Jews of Europe. It contained charts about racial feeding (feeding for starvation), accounts of the butchery of men, women and children by Nazi killer squads (Einsatzgrupen) in the Ukraine, and of the death camps which the Nazis created. As I read witness testimony, a student began to cry. She was the child of survivors. Today, we know so much more about the Holocaust and most good history teachers discuss its horrors as a way of making students aware of what is possible if they do not think and act independently. I am not certain why, but in the early 1960's, few people spoke very much about this subject. I became far more sensitive in using this material.

One memory from Eastern District which best explains why I enjoyed being a teacher, involved a student, Bruce Ellis. I do not know much about his family life, but he seemed to need someone to speak with. I used to come in early and he used to come up to my room before school began and we talked about everything. He was in my world history class, and soon after we spoke about the French Revolution, he constructed and brought to class a model of a guillotine. After we spoke about ancient Egypt, I brought in a book that my father-in-law had found and given to me about Egyptology. I encouraged him to read it and to write to its author in England. Not long afterwards a package with shards of Egyptian pottery arrived for him. Together, we brought it to the Brooklyn Museum which has a great Egyptology section. The shards were authentic. We also learned that the author of the book had died months before the shards arrived. It remained an unsolved mystery as to who had sent the shards. Before the term ended, Bruce told me that his family was moving. He brought me a gift, a single volume of the Children's Encyclopedia. It was probably his most valuable possession, and it became one of my most valuable possessions.

While at Eastern District, I became totally involved in the school. At the age of 21, I played on the faculty basketball team in the teacher student basketball game. Being only 5'7" I played hard. I remember hacking a student who came down court to score a basket. He flew into the brick wall that was only about three feet past the basket. I felt terrible. My girlfriend Judy sat with the wives, including that of the principal, Ben Michaelson. Unknown to the other women, she was only 17, younger than some of my students.

While at Eastern District, I took an examination for regular substitute teachers who had been teaching more than one year. Those who passed would be regularly appointed; the list which indicated that I passed would be posted when I was already at Jefferson.

An important development while I was at Eastern was that the city agreed to hold an election to allow teachers to elect their union bargaining agent. In that election, the United Federation of Teachers, headed by Charles Cogan defeated a more left leaning union organization. Shortly thereafter, the United Federation of Teachers staged a pre-school demonstration that led to a 10% increase in teacher salaries; from $4400 they would now start at $4800 a year. Since my father was a "union man," I reacted instinctively and joined the picket line before reporting to class.

In January of 1963, I was excessed from Eastern (told that I would lose my position at Eastern) despite the fact that a young woman hired after me was retained. The excuse given was that a teacher at Jefferson who got a U rating was transferring from Jefferson to Eastern, and I would go to Jefferson. I had taught the Regents class, and gone to Washington, D.C. without any remuneration. I thought of this as my school. Why was I excessed? There are two possible explanations. One day, as I went down stairs to the auditorium I saw a muscular male student in a verbal altercation with a female teacher. I don't know the cause, but the female teacher's verbal assault was fierce and I felt certain that the student was about to take a punch at her. I placed my arm on his shoulder and moved him into the study hall. I was called into the principal's office and reprimanded for undermining the authority of another teacher. Perhaps I should have been more conscious of that, but I was a novice. In his verbal assault, the principal referred to me as a "little boy." The female teacher involved was a very pretty red head and his "respect" for her clearly led to a dressing down that I felt could have been handled with greater tact.

A second possibility for my being excessed was that I had failed to invite any staff members to my wedding, including Frances Lief. Perhaps I was wrong. Both Judy's and my parents had very limited resources and I had never thought of inviting those with whom I worked. My father in law worked in a candy store seven days a week. My dad was certainly no capitalist. I remember bringing in some wine, liquor and cake for the department. To Lief, this may have been taken as an act of disrespect. Not long afterwards, she came into my class to observe a lesson. Something had changed. I remember that the lesson involved the Webster Hayne Debate and why it was important in American history. That debate indicated the development of sectionalism. One student played Robert Hayne, the Senator from South Carolina who stated that a state could leave the union if it felt its interests were violated. Another student, playing Daniel Webster, the Senator from Massachusetts who denied the right of any state to leave the Union. Students had been asked to do research and had been assigned roles. They did it and both quoted from the speeches of the historical figures. I was proud of my students. They had both done research and had performed with enthusiasm. Were I to observe such a lesson today, I would express my appreciation to the teacher for guiding students into doing the research, and for the participatory learning that was evident. Students will not demonstrate such efforts for a teacher who does not care. The next day, Lief entered the classroom in the middle of another lesson, handed me an observation report and insisted that I sign it immediately. Scanning the report, I noted that the previous day's lesson was rated as unsatisfactory. I refused to sign it. She did not hold a post-observation conference with me to discuss the lesson. She revised her observation report which noted that the lesson was now satisfactory, handed it to me and I signed it. By this point she had obviously decided that I would be better in another school. I was still a regular substitute and was not protected by any seniority requirement. To this day, I do not know why I was excessed.

One of my former students, now a well known historian on the life and thoughts of Ayn Rand, Chris Sciabarra once told me that when one window closes God opens another. I was sad to go, but the place to which I was being exiled was Thomas Jefferson High School, the school from which I had graduated, and a school to which I would return more than once in the future.

Chapter IV – Destiny: My return to Jefferson

The chairman of the social studies department at Thomas Jefferson High School in 1962 was Bob Shain. Outside of what I would later do as an assistant principal in charge of social studies, he is the only assistant principal for whom I ever worked who was devoted to sharing his teaching skills and focusing on the improvement of instruction. He was a master teacher and took pride in his craft. Shain had 10 new teachers that term, 9 being regularly appointed and me (still having a regular substitute license). Shain was a little shorter than me with a full head of black hair. He was a gutsy guy, who would never be afraid to tell you what he thought. The only time I ever saw him upset was after he had worked with a teacher on the improvement of instruction and then that teacher had

53

turned a deaf ear to their previous discussion. During the summer, he worked in the Catskills Mountains as a supervisor of social activities at the Windsor Hotel. He would later become the principal of Wingate High School.

At a time when the UFT had not yet won its demand that there should be compensation for every moment of required teacher time, Shain insisted that all new teachers come in early a number of days a week for instruction in methodology. I remember how he explained the importance of an evaluative aim (a question students would be required to answer at the end of the lesson), establishing instructional objectives for each lesson, how one motivates a lesson (engaging students in thinking about a problem) and the art of good questioning. I soaked it up like a sponge. I had never heard anything like this from Lief, nor in the education classes I was required to take at

Brooklyn College. I began to implement his suggestions in class, and they worked. They provided a framework for meaningful instruction. Shain published a short book on good teaching in a social studies classroom. Shain came in to observe me. He looked at my lesson plans, and I am certain that he was pleased that I was taking him seriously.

In the early 1960's, Thomas Jefferson High School, located in the Brownsville – East New York section of Brooklyn was a high performing, racially integrated school. The neighborhood, mostly Jewish and Italian had slowly begun to change. As a child, I remember playing ball with black kids outside my grandparents building. Large numbers of African Americans began coming north in the late 1950's, and two of the areas into which they moved were Brownsville and East New York. Puerto Ricans were also part of this new migration. Wooden bulletin boards with the names of students who had graduated with the highest grades lined the walls of the school. Its library was exceptional. There were portraits of past principals, some of whom had been historians and poets. I do not remember any violence at that time. After six weeks I felt at home. After two months, I was informed that a Jefferson teacher who had retired but did not have enough Jerima credits (credits for working as a substitute teacher) to retire would be returning. I would have to surrender my position. Shain asked me to sub from day to day. Remaining would have been a wiser and easier move. I told Shain that I wanted to teach and asked if he could help find me a position. Shain called a friend, a principal at Charles Sumner Junior High School in Manhattan and paved the way for me to get a position in that junior high school.

Charles Sumner was the Senator who pushed for the 13th and 14th amendments (ending slavery and granting citizenship to African Americans) after the Civil War. It is not surprising that a junior high school in this immigrant neighborhood should have born his name. Sumner had been a radical in favor of human rights, and many of the representatives elected in the urban hodge podge of lower Manhattan were progressives or socialists. The Lower East Side was always an immigrant neighborhood, its residents having disembarked through Ellis Island. Charles Sumner junior high school was located a few hundred feet from the Manhattan Bridge. One block from the school was a large Greek Orthodox Church, and two blocks west was a large synagogue. From the 1880's the immediate neighborhood had been mostly Jewish and Italian. Jews had escaped the pogroms in the Russian Empire and Italians, the grinding poverty in the south of Italy. The area still contained many five and six story walk up tenements and low-income housing projects. Sumner is no longer there. It was replaced with a new modern school in what is now the heart of the Chinese section of Manhattan.

I found Charles Sumner to be both a revelation and a horror. One of the classes I was given contained mostly Chinese, Jewish and Italian students, and most of its students were excellent. Its eighth grade students were literate and learned American History on a high school level. One class was designated as the music class. Children had lessons on the outside and were part of the band in the school. In addition to music, Chinese students attended Chinese school after their regular day in public school. Their parents were intent on their children being literate in Chinese and proud of their heritage. Other classes contained students from the poorest home environments.

In these classes, there were more Latino students. Few did their homework with regularity. They had poor reading and writing skills, short attention spans and were often inattentive in the traditional learning environment. One child etched in my memory was a skinny little girl who was short, skeletally thin and missing her front teeth. I can visualize her to this day. I remember on one occasion going to the cafeteria to get food for children whom I felt were inattentive due to a lack of food. One could see the difference by looking at the children. Those in the music class were better dressed and looked like happy children.

On the first day, I was advised by my assistant principal, that the only way to control the students in the more difficult class was to put notes on the blackboards and require them to copy most of the period. This would not be the last time that I would see teachers in a difficult teaching environment kill time in this way, because they did not know what else to do. I remember telling a young Hispanic boy that I intended to call his home to inform his parents about his failure to do homework. His response was that he lived with his grandmother who spoke only Spanish, and nobody really cared if he lived or died. I called and tried to convey in my imperfect Spanish that her grandson needed assistance. She could not help. He had told me the truth and I did not know what to do.

I really was a beginner. I had only begun to employ a few of the more traditional strategies I had learned at Jefferson, but that was in a different environment. Addressing the needs of children in a tough environment first requires assessment regarding their skills. I had no idea how to begin at this time. Once one knows what children are able to do, there are many strategies that can   be employed. Appropriate level and high interest materials should focus on improving reading comprehension. Using film to engage visual learners, and today, the use of computers to locate and write about what one has learned can be of value. Strategies involving grouping can be employed. Using the diverse neighborhood of the Lower East Side as a subject should have been possible. In order to employ them, however, one has to be aware that they exist. At this point I was unprepared. I found the inability to reach these students frustrating. The assistant principal assigned to meet with the group to which I was assigned was not a social studies person, nor a person who would help. He was a fraud. On one occasion he asked me to write minutes of a meeting which had taken place at the school before I came. Sometimes I would take a day off from school. On another occasion, I went to look for a job outside of teaching. The employer asked me to make calls and set up appointments to sell insurance to medical doctors; he wanted to see how I would communicate. I succeeded in setting up a number of appointments. He offered me the job. I then told him that this was not for me. I excused myself and thanked him for his time. At the end of the year, students in my more successful eighth grade class gave me a plaque expressing appreciation for teaching them. I deeply appreciated it. With regard to the slower class, it pained me, because I knew that I had not been very successful. Leadership which focuses on improving student performance for all children, as well as teacher training and mentoring by people with the experience of teaching in a difficult learning environment are essential for improvement.

In June, Bob Shain called me and told me that there would be a position back at Jefferson in September. I was relieved. Learning I would not be coming back, I remember Gerald Cohen, a fellow teacher, a big guy with a full face and wavy hair, asking me how I could consider leaving. We had both gone to PS 191 in Brooklyn, and I had not seen him for many years. He wrestled with the boys in his class, his kids, the more difficult kids; although he also had a social studies license, he taught them math when necessary and he loved them. Race and religion did not matter a spit – white, blacks, Hispanics – he cared about them and they knew it. I wanted to be in a more academic environment and I felt no regret about leaving, but to this day I recall this teacher with great warmth. This was clearly the kind of teacher who could succeed with needier children, and could enjoy his life doing so.

In September 1964, I returned to Jefferson for the third time. Bob Shain welcomed me and I continued to observe and learn from him. He came to use me as a subject when he was training a number of teachers to take up-coming assistant principal examinations. Three or four teachers and Shain would simply come and sit in the back of my classroom and observe a lesson. They would write observation reports of my lesson and would then compare notes regarding my strengths and weaknesses. After a number of these observations, I lost all fear of being observed. I prepared, as if I was a performer, intent upon proving my prowess. This was a practice, which should exist every school – teachers observing each other, without fear, in order to improve their craft. Later, as an assistant principal I would welcome teachers to observe and discuss my lessons, and to observe each other. In many of the high schools today, which have been divided into smaller mini "learning communities," this kind of observation is not possible, given that few have subject supervisors with expertise in their respective fields.

One of my most satisfying moments at Jefferson was the effect of my having gone to the guidance counselor of a young lady in my class who was excellent verbally but who failed each written examination. I asked that she be tested. It turned out that she had a type of dyslexia, and I was advised that assistance would be provided to her. I wondered to myself how she had gone through her entire educational experience without anyone having picked up the disparity between her intellect and written expression. This too must be the responsibility of a good teacher.

A most tragic event while I was at Jefferson was the assassination of President John Kennedy. I was in room 212 when a teacher burst into my room on November 22,

65

1963, and told me that the president had been shot. We immediately turned on a portable radio and heard the reports as they came in. At the end of the day, I was on patrol in the hall with an African American teacher. Kennedy had interceded to obtain the release of Dr. King from an Alabama jail while he was running for office, and as president, Kennedy had welcomed King to the White House after the March on Washington. Kennedy was a hero in the black community. My black colleague revealed his feelings that the struggle against racism had only begun, that it would not stop with the death of Kennedy. He stated forcefully that one day even Canarsie would have blacks. Canarsie was predominantly Italian and Jewish, and white toughs were often known to give a tough time to blacks who "crossed into their turf." Many years later both East New York (in which Jefferson found itself) and Canarsie would become predominantly black neighborhoods.

In the spring, a list was posted which indicated that I had passed the regular examination which I took while still at Eastern District. I wanted to stay at Jefferson and both the principal and Shain requested my regular appointment. At this time, Jefferson was a good school. Its student population was diverse, and there was no more violence than when I was a student. My cousins, Myra and Joanie attended Jefferson while living about ten blocks away near Linden Boulevard. After three or four months without being regularly appointed, I called the personnel unit at the Board of Education. I remember getting a lady with an Irish brogue at personnel. She asked me where I would like to go if I could not be appointed to Jefferson. Remembering the Jefferson / Tilden football games while I was a student, even without knowing exactly where Tilden was, I said, Tilden. Two days later I received a letter of appointment to Tilden High School. I never learned why I had not been appointed to Jefferson. So much for bureaucracy!

Chapter V – Tilden: A wonderful school

Samuel J. Tilden High School was named after the reform governor of New York who had broken up the Tweed Ring (a Democratic Party political machine that rigged elections and dispersed city funds to loyalists). Tilden, a Democrat, ran for the presidency in 1876, received more popular votes than Republican, Rutherford B. Hayes, but lost in the Electoral College. It seems that a deal, the Wormley Agreement, had been struck between northern Republicans and Southern Democrats. The disputed electoral votes in Florida would be given to Hayes, the Republican, if he promised to withdraw federal troops from the south, thus ending Reconstruction. Had such an agreement not been made, it is possible that African Americans would have been better protected against the racist Jim Crow system and racial segregation that followed Hayes' withdrawal of federal troops from the south. It is possible that the anger which was to lead to riots in Tilden H.S., and turned it into an almost all black school in the late 1960's and early 1970's would not have taken place. So much for what ifs in history!

Tilden was an absolutely wonderful school when I reported in February 1964. It was the finest school in which I had ever taught. Just about three or four miles west of what is called the East New York section of Brooklyn, it looked like a suburb. Whereas the area around Jefferson was clearly working class, the area around Tilden was different. Its one and two family homes, small gardens and wonderful trees had been purchased mostly by people who had done a little better than their peers in East New York and Brownsville, or people smart enough to realize that they could purchase their own homes for just a few more dollars, rather than pay rent to the landlord of an apartment building. Most of the Tilden students at that time were Jewish. Many Italian and Irish kids in the area went to a nearby Catholic parochial high school. African Americans were present, but were a distinct minority. Unlike Jefferson, with its concrete sidewalks in its frontage, Tilden had a wonderful lawn filled with trees and shrubs.

When you came into Tilden you could see a difference. The halls were better lighted than at Jefferson and the marble entranceway gave one a feeling of somehow being in a better place. I asked for directions to the social studies office. Mr. Abraham Venit was the chairman. He was a tall and impressive looking man with gray hair and a pleasant smile. When I told him that I had been regularly appointed, however, he told me that I was not really needed. At times he could seem tactless. After checking

with the principal, Mr. Margolis, he accepted the inevitable.
Teachers who passed examinations under the existing merit
system were appointed to schools with vacancies. In the
cafeteria, I introduced myself to a number of teachers, one
of whom told me that I had displaced Rosemarie, a regular
substitute teacher, whose husband, John taught English at
Tilden. I was informed, I assume with an element of
humor, that Rosemarie was well endowed and that she
would be missed. So much for enthusiastic welcomes!

Tilden had a strong social studies department. There
were two female teachers, and I recall Daisy Tauber, a
lovely lady teaching economics. Dave Goldfarb, whose
facial features seemed to resemble those of an Egyptian
Pharaoh taught an elective in Ancient History. Henry
Feingold, whose family had left Nazi Germany just in time,
was completing his doctoral thesis writing a book   entitled

"The Politics of Rescue." He would soon become a professor at the City University of New York. Larry Leventhal, whose family had survived the Hungarian round up of Jews, was a tall, quirky guy who knew his world history. Maurice Tandler, a good looking man of about 30, was working on his doctoral dissertation. Vincent Flanagan, who had attended Brooklyn College when I did, was about 25 as was I. He, too, was working to complete a doctorate at the University of the City of New York. Euriel Jackson, whose first name in Hebrew meant "fear of God" was the only African American in the department. He was a tall man with graying hair. He was soft spoken and loved by his students. He had attended Columbia University. After I would later agree to teaching African American History, he confided that he had once taken courses in Jewish History. He was a fine teacher whose son attended Tilden. I can only guess what he felt later or shared with

73

his family when the racial disturbances would tear Tilden apart. I remember Israel Muraskin, an older teacher with great fondness. Muraskin had been a member of the Spinoza Society and had communicated through written exchanges many times with fellow member, Albert Einstein in the 1930's. Spinoza, a 17th century philosopher of Jewish ethnicity, along with "free thinking" Christian philosophers, shared the belief that stripped of rituals, monotheistic religious beliefs were similar at their core. Members of the Spinoza society shared the belief that proper conduct by all human beings towards each other was logical. It was an optimistic philosophy preceding the darkness of Nazism and Communism. During the depression, he had gotten a position as an elementary school teacher by going to the Democratic club house and asking for its assistance. He later taught at Tilden for many years. Muraskin gave me wonderful photographs of historic importance when he retired. Sol Seidman was a bridge master who conducted an evening at Tilden to which families of faculty members were invited to play bridge under his supervision. The principal was Abraham Margolis, a short, broad shouldered man with a full head of wavy gray hair. He walked like a person in command.

When Venit came in to observe me teaching, he saw a teacher who, after having been shaped by Bob Shain, was unafraid of being observed. I had a carefully constructed lesson plan and was slowly becoming more and more aware of the mechanics of good questioning. He was impressed. He never seriously chose to work with me on the mechanics of a lesson thereafter. He was an interesting man. He was revered in Tilden as an intellect. Venit was an active member of the American Civil Liberties Union (an organization which sees itself as the defender of the broadest legal interpretation of the freedoms protected in the Bill of Rights) and his presence commanded a kind of awe among his colleagues. Only on one occasion did I disagree with him. When the Nazis were about to march in Skokie Illinois (where many Holocaust survivors had settled), after being denied a permit to March through a black neighborhood in Chicago, Skokie had passed ordinances denying groups with "hateful speech" the right to march. The ACLU defended the Nazi Party and saw this as a free speech issue. Venit defended the ACLU position. My reaction was that violence might well be expected, and that government should prevent Nazis from marching in the United States.

Venit saw that I was methodical. He also saw my passion for our profession. In any case, when Murray Tandler, who had been close to him and was his office manager, went on a sabbatical to complete his doctoral dissertation, Venit asked me to assume Tandler's position. The major task of the office manager was to communicate with department members, solicit multiple choice and essay questions from each teacher, put together, type and prepare uniform midterm and final examinations. Uniform midterms was a way of making certain that teachers would adhere to a departmental curriculum, would pace themselves appropriately and prepare students to demonstrate mastery of both skills and content. The department essentially did what state wide Regents are supposed to do. Examinations drove instruction. The state provides guidelines in each subject, but a fine department involves its most knowledgeable teachers in developing curriculum in each subject and providing it to each teacher. A calendar of lessons is a listing of lessons by topic in numerical order; under each topic a good calendar notes the content and skills of which students should demonstrate mastery at the end of each lesson. These keys to achieving excellence should be considered by every high school that is serious about the quality of instruction. The quality of the departmental examinations at Tilden at that time was much higher than the minimum requirements students are required to meet in Social Studies Regents Examinations today. The examinations at Tilden focused primarily on students demonstrating their knowledge of history. When Venit asked me to assume this role, I considered it a compliment and accepted without hesitation. I did not think of the time it would require beyond the preparation period that I would be given to complete this work. My assignment required me to master the content of each subject, to look up questionable material, reshape many questions, and to type each examination on a blue mimeograph stencil on a standard typewriter. Each examination was then run off on a mimeograph machine, collated and stapled by department members. A special day in the week, at a specific time was devoted to teachers giving uniform examinations. The knowledge I obtained at Tilden would serve me well in the future.

Each subject was offered on a number of grade levels. There was the honor's level, regular academic and general level. This was a system with its pros and cons. Unfortunately, public education engages in a form of mass production. As noted earlier, because of my own personal experiences, I was and remain critical of a lock step tracking system. It is logical to place students with weaker reading skills in classes in which books are seemingly simpler. On the other hand, a student who may be poor in math, like me, is tracked in all his or her subjects, and is denied an opportunity to receive a higher level of instruction in a subject for which the student might have excellent skills and a deep love. At Tilden, when I was asked at times to accept a general student into my regular history class, I willingly did so. I remember such students getting grades in the 80's on the Regents examination.

At Tilden, I asked teachers whom I respected, if I could look at their lesson plans. Without any hesitation, Tandler let me look at his lesson plans. I looked at the quotations from various historians he included in each lesson, and it made me aware of a new dimension that could be employed to enrich the student learning experience. Using conflicting historical interpretations would excite student debate in my classes. In fact, knowledge of diverse historical interpretations (historiography) is what really makes history exciting. Having taken a Master's degree in American History, and having had a love for reading the newest releases of historians in American History, I included what I learned from Tandler in my own lesson plans. As an assistant principal in charge of social studies for 23 years, I often found it disturbing that most teachers were deficient in their knowledge of their own subject.

The beauty of history is found in historiography, different interpretations of similar events, seen from different perspectives. Where a teacher provides these interpretations, the students must decide which comes closest to providing the truth. Seeking to understand human behavior is really the joy of teaching history. It causes one to think.

Social studies teachers today can obtain a license having taken only a few history courses in college. If they take courses in sociology, anthropology and psychology, all considered social sciences, only a few history courses are required for a New York State license. The social sciences can enrich the teaching of history, but history remains the core subject. Courses in women's history, African American and other ethnic subjects provide important insights, but they are not inclusive.

Government grants or free courses are given to teachers who take Master's degrees in social studies education rather than in history. Most of the classes in such programs focus on educational methodology. The members of the departments of education who teach these courses are not historians. The problem is that without real in-depth knowledge of the subject or knowledge of the best sources of information of that subject, one cannot really teach that subject well. If one is unaware of the best readings, it does little good if one knows how to raise questions about a reading in the most general terms. So we have a problem. How can people with only a general knowledge of their subject be the most effective teachers of that subject? Many people bemoan the fact that most American young people do not know enough about their history or political system. One reason may be the fact that most of their teachers lack in depth knowledge of their subjects. A panacea would be requiring social studies teachers to take courses in history directly related to what they will be teaching.

Beginning in the late 1960's and 1970's, New York City, which had been administering its own subject teacher licensing examinations, and appointing people who passed those examinations based on the merit system, took steps which shortly ended its high quality program of testing and licensing. The idea that the color or the ethnic background of a teacher was more important than what the teacher knew became more important. Politicians bought the idea of cultural anthropologists that ethnic identification would produce better student performance; it was a fallacy. Many of the examinations I took and passed, first as a teacher trainer, then an as assistant principal in charge of social studies, were set aside, because of the failure of enough "minority candidates" to pass it. It is true that white teachers did not share the African American experience, but it certainly did not mean that most white teachers were bigots who would not do their best to instruct their students. I remember that most of my elementary school teachers were either German or Irish. Many may not have loved Jewish kids, but they taught us, and I was told that it was my responsibility to learn. The black demand for more black teachers, made sense on a level – given that teaching positions also meant economic benefits, but the lunacy of ultra liberals caving in to the idea that the merit system should go, put a nail in the coffin of high quality education in this city. The idea that placing a black person (many of whom came from the West Indies) in front of a class would highly motivate students to achieve, even if the person knew little of the subject, was idiotic. That however, is exactly what was done. Had this idea ever had any merit, the problems of education of which we speak today would all be gone.

Tilden in the middle 1960's was an exceptional school. I remember that each term I was given an honor's class. This was not an advanced placement class; it was only an honor's class. Each night, in American History, I assigned readings from *Great Readings in American History* by Richard Hofstadter (a professor at Colombia

University) and conflicting historical interpretations from *The American Past* by Fine and Brown. In this class, students stood and shared their answers with the class. They argued over which historical interpretation was correct. Each argument was supported by facts. It was amazing. The quality of writing was excellent. These were students who could build a country. Class sets of soft covered books containing excerpts from historical documents in both American and World History were purchased and used. Most of our students now could not read and understand those sources.

Chapter VI – Good Days at Tilden

After a few years in Tilden, I was asked if I would take over the Tilden Forum Club. The Forum Club was a student club. It elected its officers and they decided whom to invite to share their political or social ideas with interested students. Being the advisor to this club became a joy. Notables such as Herman Badillo, the congressman from the Bronx, who later ran for mayor and became the chancellor of the City University of New York, came to address our students. Paul O'Dwyer, who became head of the city council, came to Tilden. Teens, who had experienced drug addiction and others who spoke about race relations addressed students at the Forum. Teachers debated the wisdom of our increased involvement in the Vietnam War. I remember when Vincent Flanagan and I took the patriotic but naive position that the U.S. had to act to stop the spread of communism in Vietnam. Two other teachers vehemently disagreed. The activities of the Forum club became so popular that the principal permitted students programmed for a simultaneous assembly program to be excused with a pass to attend the Forum Club. With my encouragement, the excellent leadership group from the Forum was encouraged to start a publication *The Gadfly*. Student opinions regarding the turbulent 1960's, including many about the Vietnam War, were expressed in this publication. Students submitted articles that were typed onto blue mimeograph stencils; copies were later collated and stapled by students. I had fun, often playing the devil's advocate and encouraged students to take different points of view concerning subjects which were controversial. It was pure joy. The last president of the Forum, before the Tilden which I loved was destroyed was a young woman, Paula Quick. She was a middle class, African American

88

young lady. Her intent was to bring in speakers who would discuss problems of teenagers. She was a wonderful young woman. A member of the club was Alfred Sharpton. Sharpton had a big chest, and a big head. He wore a large gold chain with a large medallion of some sort on his chest. He projected well, bellowing as if preaching, regardless of the truth. On issues of race, I recall him speaking to white students with incredible sarcasm. Implying how terrible it was that at the day's end, they took the bus west to Flatbush, and he accentuated Flatbush, as if it was a dirty word, while blacks went to Brownsville. Sharpton's tone was an implication of what was to come. Yet, they were very good days. I remember Marty Karmen, a friend of mine, and I being chaperones at dances at Tilden on Friday nights. Marty was well over six feet and kids referred to him as the Jolly Green Giant. All kids seemed to get along well. At Tilden, I became friendly with Sid Royden, a kind of Renaissance Man. Having been in debt for some failed business, in addition to teaching at Tilden, Sid worked as an oil burner mechanic at night. He had a wonderful library from which I borrowed. We were part of a pinochle game that lasted more than thirty years, until his death. Elliot Salow, another teacher, eventually became supervisor of social studies at the Board of Education and later a principal. Marty, Elliot and I still play pinochle together when it is possible.

Chapter VII – A Taste of Revolution

It is hard to explain how important and fortunate I
felt to be teaching in Tilden. The staff had so many good
people. There were Friday night student dances which I
volunteered to chaperone. In 1967, following the Six Day
Middle East War, I went to the Israel Independence Day
parade with a group of enthusiastic students who were
intent upon showing their support for that tiny beleaguered
state. There were also activities involving family members.
My joy was to be met with terrible pain in the years from
1968-70.

The first signs of winds of discontent became clear
in the spring of 1967. Mr. Margolis, the principal of
Tilden, called a faculty meeting in the library. He was an
impressive man. He was short and stocky with a full head

of gray hair. In those days, principals were often treated like kings. When he came to the cafeteria, the cafeteria help came to his table and inquired what he wanted to eat. Food was then delivered to the table. The topic of the meeting in the library was how one could best teach students with skill deficiencies. Margolis may have learned that I had once taught briefly at Charles Sumner Junior High School in Manhattan. I was asked to explain what I saw and how such students could best be reached. With my limited experience and limited success in dealing with such students, there was really little I could contribute. I explained that limited reading comprehension and short attention spans were evident among such students. Margolis then announced that a new feeder pattern to Tilden had been established in which about 50% of its incoming students would be coming from Brownsville and East New York. This would not be the first time I would see a successful school undermined by decisions involving large numbers of incoming students for which there was little, if any, preparation. In September, we found out that Margolis had transferred to a high school in Queens. Before the term came to an end, Venit asked to speak with me. He asked if I would be willing to prepare over the summer a course in African American History which would be taught in September. I had come to look upon Venit as a kind of fatherly figure, and I agreed to do so. That summer, Judy and I and our one year old son went to the Catskills where I had taken the job of camp director in the White Rock Bungalow Colony. Starting with John Hope Franklin's *From Slavery to Freedom,* I took a pile of books about African American History; I read them carefully, took notes, excerpted thought provoking quotations and prepared to teach a very fine course. The focus of my course was to introduce students to aspects of the African

American experience, to changing African American thought, and to people, both white and black who had fought injustice and taken steps to help people. It was scholarly and intellectual.

Joseph Shapiro became the new principal of Tilden. Shapiro had been an assistant principal in charge of English, at Lafayette High School. He had written the song *Round and Round* for Perry Como. Shapiro was fundamentally liberal, and was unable to conceive of events that brought upheaval shortly after he arrived, and would turn his school upside down.

The early 1960's was the best time to be a teacher at Tilden. The Civil Rights movement was making progress, and most teachers and students had a liberal bent. It is always good when one seems to be on the right side of history. I felt deep pride in the quality of education at Tilden. Please forgive me for being redundant, but in truth, it was the finest school in which I would ever teach. The quality of instruction was excellent. I worked with students in developing Forum Club presentations and in publishing our *Gadfly*. One young lady brought me a flower as a symbol of "flower power." This was before the escalation of the Vietnam war, and the riots and burnings in black communities across the nation.

The assassinations of John Kennedy and Martin Luther King, the anti-war sentiments and killings of protesting anti-war students at Kent State, and race riots in cities across the nation began to change the tone of our society. Stokely Carmichael, a black student leader of the Student Non-Violent Coordinating Committee (SNCC) declared that there was no place for whites any longer in that movement. It was now about black power. Carmichael, a black nationalist, and those who followed him, either didn't know or didn't care about the whites who helped create the NAACP and Urban League or who had gone south to defend the Scottsboro Boys. Many liberal whites refused to see it, but the black agenda had changed. Many Jews refused to accept it. Because of their own tragic historical experiences, many Jews believed that racism against blacks was also their worthy cause. Many rabbis marched with Dr. King and Jewish college students provided half of all whites who went south to racially integrate busses and promote black voter registration during the civil rights era.

I'm not certain how many people realize it, but Jews paid a very high price for their support of African American civil rights. In 1939, just before the start of the Holocaust, the

Wagner-Rogers bill to admit 20,000 refugee children (mostly Jewish) was killed in a committee of Congress dominated by President Roosevelt's Democratic Party. Individual Jews had helped create the NAACP and Urban League, and now it was pay back time. The Democrats of the "solid south" were important to Roosevelt, the politician, and his failure to show any great concern for Jewish survival was also a matter of politics.

It was no longer civil rights that were the focus of African Americans in the late 1960's. The Civil Rights Act of 1964 had marked the beginning of the end to Jim Crow. The new language of African Americans was for Black Power. What this meant, was that blacks, particularly in communities where they commanded a majority, should have community control. In education, they wanted greater control of the schools. The intellectual rhetoric meant for liberals was about the need for more black role models in teaching and positions of leadership. The rhetoric of "the street" was that white teachers could not effectively teach black children. The reality involved power to control budgets and hiring. At Tilden, the race issue was introduced into every subject by Alfred Sharpton, a member of my Forum Club.

In Brownsville and East New York, the burning and looting of shops owned by small white shop owners after the death of Dr. King, had left burned out hulks along Sutter and Livonia Avenues. Fortunoff's, which had a block of stores on Livonia Avenue, and had employed many local people ceased to exist, then moved to the suburbs. The joy from looting could only be temporary as jobs and local shopping disappeared. It was the children from these areas who were to come to Tilden en-mass after 1968.

White flight, which had begun earlier in Brownsville, East New York and lower Crown Heights dramatically increased as violence became all too common.

In 1968, New York had a liberal Republican Mayor, John Lindsay. He was upper crust white Protestant, and seemed to be a very gentle man. He had been a congressman from the *silk stocking* district of Manhattan (an area containing people with significant wealth who lived in its high rises and brownstones). He was willing to experiment. Lindsay negotiated an agreement by which greater community control would be given to the black community in the Ocean Hill Brownsville section of Brooklyn. It would be an experiment in community control. Experiments were not exactly new. Since it was recognized that some schools were overwhelmingly white and others were overwhelmingly black, liberals sought means for rectifying it. Matching of schools white and black seemed to fail, as did bussing. This would be an experiment to see whether black empowerment would bring the improvements promised in the rhetoric of the street.

In the Ocean Hill experiment, Rhody McCoy was empowered to run the schools of that area, as superintendent, and to improve the quality of education. When schools opened in September, radical elements in the black community marched outside a number of schools in that district and insisted that white teachers be fired. I personally met teachers who were told that if they returned they would never see their own children again. Teachers were intimidated by a mob and prevented from assuming their positions. On one occasion, the Jewish Defense League put some Jewish toughs in the streets to protect

Jewish teachers. The United Federation of Teachers demanded that wholesale firings be squelched and that teachers be given due process (meaning formal charges for specific negative acts before they could be dismissed) according to the UFT-city contract. To pressure the city and defend its people, the UFT called a citywide strike. The president of the UFT was Albert Shanker. Shanker, the second president of the UFT, had marched for civil rights. The building that housed the UFT provided space for the office of A. Philip Randolph, who had founded the Baggage Handlers and Sleeping Car Porter's Union. It was Randolph who had threatened a march on Washington if FDR did not issue an executive order that blacks should be hired in defense plants during World War II. It was Randolph who called for the March on Washington in 1963 during which Dr. King spoke so eloquently. Shanker and Randolph were allies, but the times were changing. White teachers became the enemy, as did Jews, in particular, in many poor black neighborhoods. Loud voices in "the black street" did not recall that many Jews had put their lives on the line to improve the lives of African Americans.

Whereas the majority of teachers in New York City's pubic schools before World War II were Protestant or Catholic, Jewish young people saw teaching as a step up, and many Jewish kids of the Baby Boomer generation went into education. The Ocean Hill Brownsville disaster saw anti-Semitism raise its ugly head. New York became a racial tinderbox. The first strike lasted from the end of September until late in November. While the schools were closed, I traveled to the Bronx, first to sell National Shoes, and then to work in an office of Sears Roebuck. The strike ended in November and I briefly returned to Tilden. After a week of chaos in Ocean Hill schools, the UFT renewed its citywide strike, and this time it was to last into January 1969. While working in Manhattan, I had caught a cold, took penicillin, to which I found I had become allergic and became terribly ill. I did not go back to work until the last days of January.

The spring of 1969 brought disaster to Tilden and personal anguish to me. I do not have the data to prove it, but a plan was seemingly hatched in the black community that would involve demonstrating that local schools within range of Ocean Hill would not be allowed to function if community control in Ocean Hill was not realized. That spring at Tilden, I taught the course in African American History. Students in this course were bright and well motivated. Most students were African Americans, but there were also a number of white students. I asked each student to read a book about an important African

American or a development in history. Students read their books and reported to the class. Then something strange began to happen. Each day, after leaving my class, during what would be official class, black students held a sit-in in the center corridor. Many of them were in my class. They demanded to meet with the principal, and gave him a list of demands. The spokesman for this group was Alfred Sharpton. At the age of seven or eight, Sharpton had been made a reverend by the laying on of the hands by Baptist Bishop Washington in Manhattan. He and his mother had moved to Brooklyn after a family break up. He was a heavy set kid with broad shoulders and a sizable Afro. Sharpton, though careful not to be tied to any act of violence or violation of regulations, would be the spokesman. The first demand of the principal was that there should be an African American club. Shapiro called upon Venit, Eurial Jackson and myself to render our opinions. Jackson and I opposed the idea of a separate club. We said that the Forum club offered an opportunity to debate all issues. Shapiro ignored our recommendation and granted their demand. The following week, during an extended official period the African American club met in the music room. In marched half a dozen young men in Black Panther uniforms holding African American flags. The red, black and Green flags became prominent in the nationalist, "back to Africa" movement led by Marcus Garvey in the 1920's. A female black teacher was their faculty advisor (each club had to have an advisor). Random acts of violence against white students began to occur. As I passed through the cafeteria, I witnessed one little white girl having cake dumped on her head. I pulled her out. During an assembly program in which black students were doing African dances, a white boy got up to leave; he was assaulted.

A few weeks later, while on the first floor, I became aware that most black students were going to the auditorium. Being the teacher of African American History gave me easy access. I was not the enemy. When I got there, I heard a student shouting that the paraprofessionals (these were community people hired to assist teachers for which there was a program for college advancement) had guns. This was planned incitement to violence. I went up quickly and told Venit what I had seen and heard, and asked him to call Shapiro. While we were speaking, black students ran through the halls of the first floor setting fire to bulletin boards. Police were called. Thugs who created havoc remained in the rear, and police struck an innocent black little girl whom I ended up driving home.

The events of this day were not spontaneous. Outside forces had directed these events. I recognized at least one of the agitators, who incited the riot, as a former black student who had graduated from Tilden the previous year. That day, Shapiro called a faculty meeting in the auditorium. As he assured teachers that all would be well, the beautiful curtain that covered the entire stage of the beautiful auditorium went up in flames. This was the beginning of a period in which I felt my guts burning. I was teaching the African American History course. I was a supporter of equal rights for all but this was different. I was angry at what I saw happening. Knowing that I was teaching African American history, a few teachers asked what I was teaching "them." I was angry as hell seeing white kids being set upon for no reason or the beautiful school, in which I felt so much pride being torn apart. The eventual effect of what began that spring led to Tilden becoming an all black school within a few years. As Tilden went, so did East Flatbush; within a short time, it became a virtually all black neighborhood. As for me, I wanted to get out. Two new schools were opening and were looking for teachers. John Dewey High School was an experimental school opening in Coney Island, no more than a few miles from where I lived. One day I called Dewey and asked for the social studies department. I spoke with Saul Bruckner, the chairman of the history department. He asked that I come in for an interview and I did. He asked to see my lesson plans for African American History. He offered me a job and I accepted.

It is interesting that Tilden is where Alfred Sharpton set out on a path that would eventually lead to his being seen by many as the most important African leader in our society. I am no fan of Alfred Sharpton. His career was filled with acts of social terrorism, all of which began at Tilden. After I left, I learned that he had written an article called "Bagel Genocide" in the *Gadfly*, the publication I had created. It was done with the permission of the principal as a free speech issue. Its theme was that Jewish teachers were committing genocide against the minds of black students. This was the beginning of an illustrious career for "Reverend Al" as he is generally addressed on WMSNBC-TV. Sharpton would incite a mob of African Americans to violence in Crown Heights, Brooklyn, against "the Jews" after an automobile accident in which the motorcade of an orthodox Jew accidentally killed a black child. His taunt was that the police were preferential to Chassidic Jews. An African American youth stabbed a student at the Chasidic Lubavich seminary to death, and an Italian man with a beard, mistaken for a Jew, was killed on Eastern Parkway. Jews hid in their homes during a number of days in which acts of violence were taking place. Mayor David Dinkins, the first African American to serve as mayor, and his police commissioner, seemed paralyzed and did not fully deploy the police in that part of Crown Heights for a number of days. Had a white leader incited a white mob to act as Sharpton did, he might have been indicted for inciting to riot. Sharpton was like Teflon. Perhaps this was the time that he admittedly worked as an FBI informant. Does one recall how he nearly destroyed the life of an innocent law enforcement official in Newburg, New York, accusing him of rape in the Tawana Brawley case? After years, Brawley admitted that her story was fictitious. Many times, the federal government accused Sharpton of tax evasion, but fires destroyed all records and Sharpton would always claim that he was penniless and that all he had really belonged to his action committee. Sharpton would be given federal money to run for president of the United States, and under President Obama, he would be made an official consultant, along with Newt Gingrich, of all educational programs in the United States. In 2014, Mayor DiBlasio in New York called upon Al Sharpton to advise him on how police and other issues should be resolved. I was an eye witness to the beginning of the success story of Alfred Sharpton, the reverend who became "too big to fail."

An interesting question is who or what killed Tilden? Was it the liberals who surrounded Mayor John Lindsay, who wanted instantaneous racial integration? Who directed that feeder patterns (50% of incoming students would come to Tilden from Brownsville and East New York all at once) change so rapidly? Who organized young African Americans and used Al Sharpton to tear apart the school? Who is accountable? Was it the inability of an old style liberal principal to have criminals arrested? In any case, it was with pain and deep regret that I wanted out of

Tilden.

Chapter VIII – The Dewey Experiment

I taught at John Dewey from 1970-1986. That is a long time and a major part of my life. John Dewey, with a large campus and athletic fields was meant to be an experimental high school. John Dewey, for whom the school was named, was an educator who reasoned that ways had to be employed to motivate a love of learning for its own sake, minus much of past rigidity in education. Given the chaos in so many schools in the late 1960's, Dewey was meant to be an alternative to what existed. The school was open to all applicants, citywide. Its aim was to encourage students to achieve maximally in a non-competitive environment. The Dewey experiment called for a planned school in which 25% of the students admitted each term would be above grade in their reading levels, 50% on grade level and 25% below. Its aim was to program students into the same classes without tracks. Interaction, led by those in the upper levels would hopefully motivate those below.

More ambitious students could take and complete units of work prepared by coordinators though independent study or students could create their own units of independent study. An independent study unit required a student to do research, write a paper about the subject and explain to the coordinator of that subject what had been learned. It was my pleasure to witness one student, Errol Giray, create seven or eight independent study units on his own in science, for which he received course unit credit. Students could advance as rapidly as they could complete the work.

Grouping, as a methodology was encouraged in classrooms. Students would be given problems to research, debate and draw conclusions. Each group would select a chairperson and secretary. Selected students from each group would then debate their peers in other groups about their solutions to given problems. Grades at Dewey were to be non-numerical (ME for mastery with excellence, M for mastery, MC for mastery but conditional and R for repeat). No one would bear the stigma of failure. The school was to be non-competitive. It had no teams that would compete in inter-mural competitions with other high schools. There were to be five cycles in a year, as opposed to two semesters, and each class would be for approximately six weeks. In social studies, students would select a required number of mini courses from a larger number in a general subject area (for examples, which regions of the world to study). Dewey even had an auto shop open to male and female students. Teachers developed the mini-courses in a special summer for teacher training. Dewey had wonderful Art and Music programs. Saul Bruckner, the social studies chairman, introduced me to the principal, Josh Siegel when I came for an interview. Siegel had been in on the planning and initial design of the school. He was a young man, perhaps in the early forties, had an open collar and appeared dynamic. When I began to teach in September, he was no longer there. I believe he accepted a higher position outside of the city. Sol Levine became the new principal.

Saul Bruckner was a very bright man with a near photographic memory. I once asked him to look at a reading. He scanned the page in seconds and could recall what he read. As Assistant Principal in charge of social studies, he could at times be described as strange. A teacher in the department told him how his little girl had been born with a heart defect that morning; he observed his class in the afternoon. On one occasion, I confided that I had been up most of the night with a sick child and I too was observed that day. Yet, he was a fine administrator, but at times, something in his behavior was missing. During the summer of 1970, all new teachers met over a six-week period, wrote mini-courses and demonstrated their skills with students in summer school classes. The training, especially in writing mini-courses and grouping was excellent.

The social studies teachers at Dewey, in retrospect, were a highly ambitious group. Bruckner, Pero, Fisher, Sigalakis and Smith were all to be principals. Bromberg was to become a director of social studies for the Board of Education. Others, including Edelman, Wolfson and

Cabeza were all strong personalities. I too, knew that I was good. Fisher had worked for Bruckner at Bushwick and Pero with him at Lincoln. He saw both as special and they were to benefit from their previous association.

In September 1970, I was ready to go. One of the reasons that Bruckner hired me was my experience in teaching African American History. I was given two classes. Little did I know that a decision somewhere had been made that white teachers should not be allowed to teach that subject. I had excellent lesson plans, reading lists and the materials that proved successful at Tilden. I knew my subject well. Each day, shortly after I began to teach, a handful of students began to act out, call out and prevent the lesson from succeeding. One student, John, got up to dance. I told Bruckner but nothing was done.

I spoke with John in the hall. He seemed normal. He explained that his behavior would be what it was in class. Bruckner, who was bright, came up with an idea. He gathered these students and promised to offer an African American History course that they would write. Of course, it was not written, nor was African American History to be taught again at Dewey during the next 15 years that I was to be at Dewey.

The first elective I introduced at Dewey was entitled *Anatomy of Revolution*. The very late 1960's saw a lot of talk about revolution in the U.S. There were the often violent anti-Vietnam war protests, and the rhetoric of black militants and the Black Panther Party. The course I introduced, using Crane Brinton's book, *Anatomy of Revolution*, compared the causes, phases and effects of the English, American, Russian and Chinese Revolutions.

Among the materials I gave out were hypothetical situations of societies in which unrest existed. I loaded the reading so that there were as many factors in those societies which could have prevented revolution as there were leading to it. In groups, students drew conclusions, and appointees from students debated in front of the class. Questions of speakers from the audience followed. Later, one of my students, who attended West Point, returned to Dewey for a visit and told me how important the insights in that course had been to him.

"TV and the Popular Mind" was another course I introduced. It focused on rules set by the FCC governing the operations of television and other mass media in our society. Students then moved on to produce their own news programs in our studio. A studio had been constructed for this purpose. Using simple cameras and a mixer, students were excited by this course. In a follow up elective I developed, students studied documentaries and propaganda films. They realized the difficulty in sometimes distinguishing between them. They then produced their own mini Documentary and Propaganda shorts.

After the demise of African American History, Bruckner asked if I would teach a course on Jewish History, and I did so. In this course, I required each student to teach about events affecting the Jewish people during a particular time period. I sat with kids and taught each how to design a lesson plan, how to motivate a lesson and question.

One day, I was asked if I would teach a course about the Holocaust. This was a serious and painful subject. This followed the 1973 Middle East War, in which Israel was surprised by the attack by Egypt and Syria on Yom Kippur, and many feared for the survival of the Jewish state. The subject of the Holocaust was not one about which most Jews would speak before this time. Not only was it painful, but I believe that few Jews were willing to speak about it because it revealed a time of relative helplessness. People do not enjoy feelings of helplessness. The willingness to speak about it now came from a kind of anxiety that this could happen again to the Jewish people if they did not speak out. Believing I would be doing something of value, I agreed to develop and teach a course about the Holocaust. Teaching about the Holocaust over the past forty years has made people more aware of what is possible in our world, but it has not made people any more humane, nor has anti-Semitism disappeared. Given the freedom to create, Dewey, certainly during its early years, was a special place.

Studying and teaching about the Holocaust was to become my passion for many years. I chose dozens of volumes I felt necessary to read before I could develop a curriculum for teaching this difficult subject. I read personal accounts and the accounts of historians like William Shirer (author of *The Rise and Fall of the Third Reich and Berlin Diary*) and of Nora Levin who wrote the book entitled *The Holocaust*. The writings of Elie Wiesel, Alexander Donat, and Simon Wiesenthal were among the books read. Nightmares came regularly. Normal people still cannot explain how the people in one of the most civilized nations in Europe accepted the unquestioned leadership of a man, whose world view was demonic, and were able to mass murder millions of people, Jews and non-Jews, including a million and a half Jewish children.

Each lesson taught posed a question as to whether each factor that made the Holocaust possible could be found within our own society. Students discussed the extent to which previous Jewish history (Jews having been accused collectively of Deicide – the killing of God – in earlier Christian teaching) was responsible for the mindset that resulted in the mass murder of Jews. Students explained Nazi ideology, the idea that racial struggle was the most important idea in history, justified with pseudo scientific one liners from social scientists who claimed that evolution (as suggested by Darwin) produced superior and inferior races, and that superior could elevate human kind by eliminating the "inferior." We studied Nazi propaganda (the use of 20th century mass media), laws, technology, and psychology and drew conclusions as to how each of these factors made such horrors possible. Students concluded that it was important for Americans to be aware of how

124

each of these factors could be misused, and it was important to prevent that from every happening in our society. By reading accounts of survivors, and hearing them speak, students realized that smuggling in food to feed a child when in a ghetto qualified as resistance. They studied accounts of those non-Jews who saved their Jewish neighbors (naysayers – those who neither assisted the Nazis nor were silent) and discussed the special qualities of these people. Most disturbing to students was the inaction of the U.S., as a nation, in any serious effort to save Jews. The course became the singular most desired social studies course in John Dewey High School. As a mini-course, it was offered every other cycle for eight years, the remaining years I was at Dewey.

In 1974, I applied for a mini-grant from the New York State Department of Education for a project in oral history. Having tape recorders and cameras allowed selected students and myself to go into the homes of survivors of the Holocaust and American war veterans who liberated such death camps as Dachau and videotape their accounts. Dr. Jonas Faine, who was an officer with Eisenhower's command in England, described on audio tape how he put his head into a box car filled with the dead at Dachau, and how he was reminded of the smell of human flesh every time he attends a barbecue. This was the same protein burning that we in New York smelled after the terrorist attack on 9/11 on the World Trade Center. Chris Sciabarra, Don De Lorenz and a few of my other excellent students took part in interviews. A small videotape collection began to develop. The idea of creating a Holocaust Center and Center for the Study of Humanity developed in my mind. I wrote to war veterans groups, and many, especially the Jewish War Veterans, provided

126

funding for the purchase of books related to this subject. Nell Miller, the head librarian, strongly supported our efforts. Students helped research for articles and a microfiche collection was assembled. Photographs from the New York Historical Society were developed, enlarged and placed around a small section of the library. The time came when the center was dedicated. Notifications were sent to veteran's groups, and to local newspapers. An invitation was sent to the Armenian Prelate (Armenian Christians had been mass murdered in the declining Ottoman Empire during World War I. Hitler once commented, "Who remembers the Armenians."). I had no idea that the Dewey Cafeteria would be packed. Many of those who attended were either Holocaust survivors or children or survivors. Mrs. Esther Wagner, wife of a rabbi, a survivor who had been videotaped, attended. Students, including Chinese, Italian, Jewish and African

American took the microphone and explained what they had learned in studying about the Holocaust. The center developed an extensive library which provided readings for students taking the elective.

The following year, a conference about the Holocaust was held at John Dewey High School. It was sponsored by the UFT and Association of Teachers of Social Studies. The keynote speaker that evening was Vladka Meade, a survivor, who had been a courier between the Jews in the Warsaw Ghetto and friendly underground fighters in the "Aryan" section of Warsaw.

Jews had made up one third of the population of Warsaw, the Capital of Poland, in 1939 prior to the Nazi invasion of Poland and the start of World War II. In September 1939, Nazi Germany attacked Poland from the

West. Not long afterwards, the Soviet Union, which had signed a non-aggression Pact with Nazi Germany, attacked from the East. Poland surrendered. Warsaw was occupied by the Nazis. A systematic step by step Nazi plan for the extermination of the Jews of Poland was implemented. The Jews of Warsaw were compelled to move to a walled off area, a ghetto. Half a million Jews were isolated behind its walls. Forced labor and a starvation diet were imposed. Before the deportations to the Nazi extermination camp of Treblinka began, hundreds of thousands of Jews had already perished from typhus and starvation.

Ms. Meade addressed a subject others usually avoided. She spoke of what resistance meant in the Warsaw Ghetto, how smuggling food, feeding children, teaching school (which was forbidden), in addition to Jews in the underground, were all important forms of resistance. They were all forms of heroism. There was praise rather than shame for those who had struggled to survive, and she left her audience understanding something that few had considered before. My dad, whose sister and her children were murdered by the Nazis, came and peered deeply at the artifacts shown in display cases. I did not know how to interpret the look on his face. Among the artifacts was a Jewish star donated by my neighbor, Henry Goodheim, a French Jew, who was hidden by good Christian people but whose mother was caught in a round up of Jews in Paris and who died in Auschwitz. His contribution had been his own star of David, which was meant to have been sewn on his clothing. It was a memorable evening.

A year later, recognizing the importance of my work at Dewey, I received the John Bunzel Memorial Award from the United Federation of Teachers and

Association of Teachers of Social Studies. John Bunzel, an excellent social studies chairman had unfortunately passed away the previous year.

The John Dewey Holocaust Center and Center for the Study of Humanity, located in our school library, became a place to which students from elementary and junior high schools were to come in the future. Students who had completed the elective and worked with me in a training course received the visiting groups, showed them parts of videotaped interviews and guided them in a follow up discussion.

I had no idea that immersing myself in this subject would involve me so deeply in Holocaust education. I learned from the Jewish Survivors and Fighters Organization that the National Jewish Resource Center, headed by Yitz Greenberg was producing a series of videotapes about the Holocaust. I called and spoke with Dr. Greenberg. Our discussion led him to ask me to write lesson plans to accompany each of the Holocaust related videotapes that the Center was to release. In return, I would be allowed to keep the tapes that would be used to enrich my lessons.

It is interesting that so much had been filmed, some by the victims and other scenes by the Nazis. Students were able to see the synagogues burning on Kristalnacht (November 9 and 10 1938 when Nazi Party bands were given a free hand to destroy Jewish life in Germany and Austria) and heard accounts of survivors who described the burning of synagogues, and its effects upon their own families. Others captured life in the Warsaw Ghetto, the shooting and murder of Jews in the Ukraine, and one videotape contained photographs of Jewish resistance fighters in the forests of Belarus. One of the people deeply involved in the project of the National Jewish Resource center was a nun, Mary McGlynn, who was as committed as anyone involved. I felt honored to be working with such people.

I was asked to represent the Center at a meeting for teachers of the subject at the Massachusetts Institute of Technology in Cambridge Massachusetts. At MIT, I sat next to noted Harvard professor and historian Dr. Eric Goldhagen. We were both called upon to explain how we thought this subject should be taught. I considered it an honor to have had this opportunity. I was contacted by Professor Braham at the Graduate Center of the University of the City of New York and was asked to teach a course for teachers and educators at its Eisner Institute for

Holocaust Studies. Given what I was doing at the Institute, I contacted the Anti-Defamation League and asked if they would publish a book of the lessons I was providing to educators in the Eisner Institute. In 1983, after many years of work, *Classroom Strategies for Teaching About the Holocaust* was published by the ADL (Anti-Defamation League of B'nai Brith). I was paid $200 for years of labor and there were many reprintings of this books which the ADL sold. It was a labor of love. There were no royalties. My book contains ten lessons, and materials (readings and graphics) necessary for the inclusion of the study of the Holocaust within existing world history curriculum. Many teachers throughout the country used the lessons provided.

I considered Dewey my home, and was caught up in my own idealistic world; I was unable to see many of its faults.   Then suddenly something personal happened.

Solomon Schechter Hebrew High School in Brooklyn, which my oldest son attended, collapsed. Conflict among those who provided essential funding led that school to close its doors. I approached Jack Metzger, the assistant principal in charge of guidance, a very nice man, explained my situation, and he immediately told me that I could register my son at Dewey. Suddenly I was not only a teacher, but also the parent of a student at Dewey. My son had previously attended the Bialik Hebrew Day School (K-8). Work was advanced and he was able to take not only the Algebra Regents in grade 8 but the Geometry Regents in Grade 9 (in the Solomon Schechter High School which was upstairs). In both of those examinations he received grades of over 90. Now he came to Dewey. He joined the math team and was taking pre-calculus. However, he was told that he also had to complete five cycles of integrated math (a method of teaching each of the mathematical

135

subjects combined; a system ended in NY in 2008). He had taken algebra and geometry as separate subjects. He had never learned Integrated Math. Fate would have it that he had a teacher who decided my son was an idiot, and after one cycle, insisted he be made to take that subject in seven cycles, with slower students. The result was that he was dropped from pre-calc, where during the first cycle he had done well. I told him to see the chairman of the math department, a man with whom I had been cordial, and I told him I had confidence that his problem could be resolved. The chairman expressed no interest in helping him. My son went back to his integrated math class and arrived a few minutes late. The teacher would not open the door and admit him, and he later told my son that he would be failed on the quiz given because he was not present. I went to see the chairman, who said, "Your son thinks that he is better than he is. He even went to the chess club and asked to challenge the best player." The implication was that there was something wrong with my son. My son took the seven cycle integrated math course and never took another math course again. Later in Brooklyn College, he was the president of the chess club, hired a Russian Grand Master as a coach and the Brooklyn College chess team defeated Harvard and won national recognition.

Given his problem with math, I advised him to speak to his guidance counselor. His classes were such that he arrived only minutes before his counselor's lunch period. His counselor was about to slam the door in his face when he recognized his last name and relented. This genius programmed my son for an elective in ancient history that I was teaching for Long Island University college credit. I asked him to urge Barry to take an elective in another area. He refused. My son, who later became a lawyer, could be provocative. His philosophy was conservative, while many of the kids in Dewey were from Park Slope were liberal. They were at war in Advanced Placement American History and this continued in my class. It was a very difficult term for me.

On one occasion we received a letter from the attendance office at Dewey that my son had been cutting class. He had been marked present in official class but absent in all subject classes. My wife went to see his homeroom teacher, Kobliner, a few days later on open school night. She informed him that he had been absent that day and she had taken him to the doctor. Kobliner, quizzical about speaking to the parent of a student not in his subject class, insisted that he had been right. My wife, who was also a teacher, told him that she had heard that students often took attendance in his class, and that his

138

failure to attend to this legal document himself could result in his dismissal. The teacher relented and the present was changed to an absence. By following my son's activities, I also learned how fine a teacher Stan Bloomfield, who taught Russian literature was, and how wonderful the efforts of teachers involved with the repertory company were. The chairman of the English Department was Joseph Zogby and the repertory company was his baby. In the cafeteria we used to speak cordially over a cup of coffee. I remember him asking me about my own values. Not long afterwards he came out and publicly admitted that he was gay. We live in an interesting world. He passed away a relatively short time later. He was a nice man.

My son took a boatload of units on independent study and graduated after one and half years at Dewey. My experience as a parent had given me a more realistic perspective. In my 'fantasy land" of hard work, and befriending many really good people, I had failed to see the complete reality. The school was hardly as perfect as I thought it was. What did I learn from the experience of having my son in the school in which I taught? I learned that teachers and counselors whom I believed were committed to helping children could be destructive. I learned that a school is only as good as its individual teachers and learned that parents must be involved if for no other reason than to defend the interests of their children.

Chapter IX– Racism and Nepotism

The social upheaval following events at Ocean Hill Brownsville, led politicians to accept the idea that appointing more minorities to administrative positions was necessary, if for no other reason than to prevent what had taken place in Tilden. In retrospect, it is interesting to speculate whether it was fear by people in the establishment, or ideology, that led to an end of the merit system. Supervisory examinations were given but their grades were never published and their results were set aside. While at Dewey, I passed an examination as a Teacher Trainer in Junior High School, but those who passed were never appointed. Not only had I passed a written examination for this license, but I had taught a lesson judged by two supervisors after having been given an hour to prepare. I passed examinations, twice, as an

Assistant Principal in charge of social studies in high schools, but they too were set aside. The reason openly given was that too few minorities passed the examinations. It was stated that these exams were culturally discriminatory. In simple terms, it accepted the premise that there was a "white culture" that had been inaccessible to blacks, and that such examinations had been unfair. In the absence of appointments under the merit system (if you had passed you were appointed to wherever there was an opening), principals (who often got their positions by belonging to a particular ethnic organization) selected their friends. Those people in turn selected their friends.

Saul Bruckner was selected as principal at Edward R. Murrow High School. He helped secure the assistant principal position for Larry Pero at Dewey. Having obtained a New York City administrative license, I asked

Bruckner if the position of AP social studies was open at Edward R. Murrow. All along it was suspected that he would take Norman Fisher, whom he had brought with him from Bushwick High School to Dewey. Fisher was intelligent, and he would prove himself far more politically astute than I was. Yet, having once demonstrated his skills as a teacher in a classroom for members of our department, he was no more than an average teacher. Bruckner assured me the position was open. I arrived at Murrow for an afternoon interview and Bruckner took me into a book room and asked me a number of questions. The next day, in the teacher's lounge, Fisher told us how parents and other supervisors asked him questions in his interview. It was a painfully bad joke. Years later, at a United Federation / Association of Supervisors of Social Studies conference, I asked Bruckner why he had perpetrated such a fraud. He turned to me and said, "You understand don't you?" Fisher became Bruckner's assistant principal in charge of social studies at Murrow and then became principal at Madison H.S. a few years later. As principal at Madison, he took Bill Sigelakis, a teacher at Dewey with him as his assistant principal in charge of social studies.

Sol Levine left to become principal of Beverley Hills High School in California. After Levine left, there was an interim acting principal, who was not given the position. Lew Smith, a former social studies teacher who had been my colleague in the social studies department at Dewey, had briefly been an assistant principal outside of Dewey, and now returned as principal. Smith called an assembly of teachers, the announced purpose of which was to explain our ideas as to how education could be improved at Dewey. Teachers hailed this new democracy as sign of teacher empowerment. Two hours into the new school year, he called Jay Sachs to his office. Smith and Sachs had once had a near violent disagreement when both were teachers. Sachs had both regular Chemistry and Physics licenses. He was a regular teacher with more seniority than many other teachers in the science department. Smith told Sachs that he was being excessed to another school. To do this, Smith had to excess all others with less seniority than Sachs. Smith destroyed an excellent science department at Dewey in order to "screw" Sachs. Later, Smith was forced to resign when the Board of Education learned that Smith had used the labor of his students to repair his brownstone in Park Slope. During my remaining years in Dewey, the school's science department was always weak, containing many part time substitute teachers.

Dr. Michael Costello, who served many years at the Central Board of Education, was then appointed   principal.

The Assistant Principals seemingly hated him. He had not been school based and they seemed to resent *this interloper*. My experience with him was excellent. He had coffee in the morning and spoke openly with teachers in the cafeteria. Explaining that I wanted to become an AP, and that many of the appointive examinations I had passed were set aside for being "culturally biased," he advised me to speak with Brooklyn High School Superintendent Martin Ilivicky, and I did. Costello was forced out, but since he held the only state license as supervisor of testing, he was appointed to that position at the Board. Mike called me to tell me that an exam I passed was finally going to be approved, and I should take the two special education courses required for that position. I did so and the examination was approved on the very last day of the courses.

With Michael Costello leaving, and an interim failing in his efforts, Larry Pero was made principal. I had recently had my book published and I was the only one who had a New York City license to be assistant principal in charge of social studies in the department. Pero asked Barry Nelson to be his acting assistant principal. He announced this at a social studies department meeting. He could have asked people who were interested to apply. He obviously chose the person with whom he was most comfortable. At the same time he announced Nelson's appointment, he also announced that visitors from other schools were planning to come and visit my Holocaust class. This was one of the few times I lost it. In front of the department, I stated that I had both the license and had recently been published. With regard to the supposed visit, I told him to go and fuck himself.

I can't be certain as to why I remained on the outside. I had never become one of the boys whom they took along for the ride. I was devoted to my family first and then to my job. I really believed that hard work would ultimately be recognized and rewarded. I was naïve. I never realized the importance of networking. Those who selected each other often used to go out to eat in Arab restaurants in down town Brooklyn Endless bottles of consumed wine filled their table on occasions when I joined them. Perhaps they could see the resentment on my face when I paid "my share" of a huge wine bill for wine I barely touched. On at least one occasion, the boys enjoyed porno flicks during Regents week and I felt no need to go.

I went to see Superintendent Martin Ilivicky whose office was at Edward R. Murrow High School. I explained my desire to become an AP. I showed him my book and other work I had done. Two weeks later, I entered my classroom at 7:30 A.M. and Illivicky was already there to observe me. He observed a lesson in which students were divided into groups and asked which of the approaches described on a worksheet they would have taken had they been African Americans in the age of Jim Crow. The next week, I was contacted and asked if I would take the position of Assistant Principal of Social Studies at Thomas Jefferson High School. After giving it a good deal of thought, I responded that if it was a regular rather than an interim appointment, I would be interested in taking it. A small number of people were interviewed and I was appointed.

By the time I left Dewey, it was no longer the shining experiment, the "city on the hill" that it had been in 1969 and 1970. The Board of Education made decisions that altered its fundamental plan. As long as 25% of its students were above average, 50% average and 25% below, students at the bottom could be motivated to improve their performance. First, because it had a campus, the number of special education students was significantly increased. Then, admission procedures were changed. In New York City, students applying for high schools had been given the opportunity to state their preferences. Dewey had generally accepted students for whom Dewey was their first choice. Such students were willing to travel significant distances by train and/or bus. Many came from Park Slope, Midwood and all other parts of the borough. Being located near Coney Island, which was primarily African American, Dewey had a significant African American population. The new admission procedures required Dewey to accept students for whom Dewey was their second or third choice. The result was that more children came from economically depressed areas and had poorer academic skills. Like Gresham's law in economics, bad money drives out good. Children in mixed classes who performed well noted that a majority of their classmates could not read well, and that the quality of instruction declined. Their siblings no longer applied for Dewey. The top slowly disappeared as the students who came to Dewey from more middle class sections of the borough stopped coming. The Dewey experiment began to wither. Recently, Dewey was divided into mini-schools, the idea that smaller and more focused schools would motivate students with serious deficits. Dewey, in its hay day, had children commuting from all over the borough; it has now become a predominantly "minority school." Who made the decisions that affected the nature of the school? Not surprisingly, no one seems to have taken the credit for the changes that killed the Dewey experiment.

Chapter X – Returning Once Again to Jefferson

I was appointed assistant principal in charge of social studies at Thomas Jefferson High School in February 1986. Thomas Jefferson High School was very different in 1986 from what it had been in 1963.

Whereas it had been a racially and ethnically integrated school for working class children, it now contained a student population of about 1500, about 85% African American and 15% Hispanic. Its students came mostly from families that were poor.

The East New York / Brownsville area had changed dramatically. Whereas Sutter Avenue and many of the other side streets had once been filled with small retail shops, there were now many empty stores. The stores on Livonia Avenue, including those of Fortunoffs, had been burned out following riots after the death of Dr. King. When I had left in 1963, a kosher delicatessen existed on the corner of Pennsylvania Avenue and an active candy store existed on the other side of the street. They were gone. There was, however, a bodega (a Latino grocery) across the street from the school. The area had a terribly high crime rate, and many a day I lowered the shades in my small office when I heard shots from the low income housing project across the street in the back of the school.

Disputes among students were often solved by violence. Interestingly, more of the fights involved girls fighting over relations with "a man" whom each claimed as her own. To prepare for their fights, girls took off their ear rings and their blouses, fighting in their bras.

One young man in my class was out for about two weeks. He was a handsome young man, and was very bright. I asked why he had been absent. He unashamedly explained that he had been in jail for a shooting related to the selling of drugs. Here was a student whom one could swear would do well in any middle class school, yet his future was questionable.

A summer program I was supervising at Jefferson was meant to improve the reading comprehension and writing skills of entering ninth grade students. As an incentive for attending, students were also taken on trips. One of our trips was to the aircraft carrier, The Intrepid, in New York Harbor. Students were required to climb ladders to reach the deck. Suddenly I noticed one little girl, age 15 or 16, climbing down the ladder with a large belly.   She was pregnant, in her seventh or eighth month. I panicked. We all returned to school safely. The next day she introduced me to her boyfriend, who was no taller than five feet and could have weighed no more than 90 pounds. Children were raising children. If the above brief accounts have an element of humor, events of November 1991 and February 1992 were anything but humorous. On November 26, 1991, a student shot and killed another student in school and wounded a teacher. In February 1992, on the day Mayor Dinkins was scheduled to visit the school, two students were shot to death down the hall from my office. Both were shot in the head in execution style. I heard the defense invoke the claim that had the shooter not taken out his victims, he would have been killed. A police officer was assigned to the school full time, and students entered after showing their ID cards and passing through metal detectors. In theory, steps were taken to provide for security at Jefferson. In reality, there were multiple doors on the north and south sides of the building which could be opened to an intruder from the inside. Fire department regulations prohibited them from being chained during school hours.

The principal of Thomas Jefferson when I reported in February 1986, was Barbara Ford. She was a black woman in her fifties whose face could demonstrate stress, but who was honest and could muster a big smile. She spoke honestly and I could go into her office, sit down and feel comfortable after being disturbed by some act of senseless violence in the halls. We didn't have to say a word. We understood each other. I liked her. She knew I would be trying to bring some semblance of sanity to my own department, and she and others were probably somewhat surprised that I would willingly come to

Jefferson from John Dewey High School. Not long afterwards, Barbara Ford introduced me to the new Superintendent of the Brooklyn High Schools Superintendency. Dr. Joyce Coppin was a black woman, who replaced Ilivicky after he retired. She visited my class, and all students participated in a lesson. This was an achievement and I felt proud of my students. Her reaction was mixed. She seemed to have expected more sophisticated responses and I told her that students participating in this class were a plus. She came to my office and saw the calendars of lessons I was preparing for teachers and piles of homework sheets I was then working on producing for students. She stated her approval. Somewhat disturbed by her mannerisms earlier, I told her that they were indeed very good. Despite our cold beginnings, we later developed respect for each other. During the summer of 1986, Ford transferred to Rikers

Island (a prison high school), after probably having been given "a choice" she could not refuse. Her replacement was Carol Beck.

Beck could have been a news media darling. Beck was a tall, very good looking black woman. Her husband was a Jewish white guy who taught at Lafayette high School. If I seem cynical about him, it is because after each killing at Jefferson, he would appear, camera in hand to record his wife speaking to large student audiences and introducing black leaders, one after the other. Beck could have been featured in a movie. What Jefferson needed was a serious educator intent upon preparing her students to make it in a very tough environment!

During my first meeting with her, she informed me she had fired a regular substitute teacher in social studies because she could not understand his English. He was a fine and knowledgeable teacher from Jamaica, who knew his history and whom students understood well after the first day. She had never shown me the courtesy of consulting with me about that teacher. Throughout her tenure, there was never a time when she did not have an assistant from the superintendent's office. All happened to be white women. In retrospect, Coppin must have known whom she was appointing.

Upon coming to Jefferson, I was asked to create a Law Institute and I proceeded to do so. It was named after Lloyd G. Sealy, whom I had learned was the first black police commander in Brooklyn South. On a number of occasions, I accompanied Beck to meet with parents and guidance counselors from feeder schools. I explained my expectations for our law program, and asked them   to encourage their students to attend our school. Beck would then tell them that it would be good "considering that this was still Thomas Jefferson." Her presentations left me wondering what the hell was wrong with her.

Cabinet meetings were called, and I came to a number of them prepared to discuss tough issues. In one such meeting, the assistant from the superintendent's office advised me that we were really there to celebrate Beck's birthday. I do not remember one cabinet meeting in which serious issues were discussed. Her Assistant Principal in charge of Administration was a woman, Frieda Homer. I never did understand her. When I went to her office requesting office supplies, like paper clips and rubber bands, she would extract a hand full from there desk and hand them to me. I would never receive a full package of rubber bands or paper clips from her. Each year, departmental chairpersons got an allotment with which to purchase books. Jefferson contained many transient students and the drop out rate was high. Hundreds of books disappeared each term. I would get an allotment of about $3,500. The average cost of each book at that time was about $50. Given the allotment, I could purchase no more than 75 books. I really did not know that I should have gotten a lot more money. When I later went to Westinghouse, its principal gave me $15,000 for a school with a similar student population. I found Catholic parochial schools that were willing to part with old books and I personally went to pick them up. On one occasion, I travelled to Manhattan where a school was becoming a K-8 school and was getting rid of its 9th grade social studies books. I packed my car with hundreds of books and returned to Jefferson. Given a kind of esprit de corps with the teachers in my department, Ed Seidlinger and Marty

Buchman also made such runs. All of us thought that we were doing it for the kids. How did Beck spend her money? She rented the auditorium at Lincoln Center for a graduation and a wedding hall for a cotillion for her graduates (girls wore gowns and gloves and male students wore tuxedoes). Where else it went, God only knows.

The department I came to supervise at Jefferson, contained three tenured white male teachers from a previous time and others, mostly African Americans, who held licenses as substitute teachers. The task of creating a department was not easy. Over the next few years, I hired people who were solid teachers, black and white, people who were willing to prepare carefully for their classes, and who could command the respect of their students.

One teacher, who was appointed in better days, and was a really nice man, was Stuart Rothstein. He was the UFT chapter chairman for the school. He was well liked. When I came to Jefferson, I asked him to help me develop calendars of lessons and courses of study for teachers. He tried to assist me, but having taught at Jefferson for many years, he simply didn't have the skills I had an opportunity to develop over the years. The second tenured teacher went off on tangents in each lesson observed, and only the most minimal learning took place in his classroom. I knew that he liked economics, so I programmed him for it and encouraged him to work with kids on computers in order to obtain data. Believing I could excite the third tenured teacher, I gave him an honor's class in American History. All he did was fill blackboards full of notes for students to copy, notes from a review book. A person whom Superintendent Coppin sent into the school visited his class in the afternoon. There were only a handful of students; one student ostensibly told the investigator that his teacher promised grades over 90% to students who promised not to come to class. I do not know if this was true, but he refused assistance and I was frustrated as hell. After a year, he left the system and went to work for the Immigration Service. A year and half after I came to Jefferson, both Rothstein and the second teacher transferred to Midwood High School. I regretted having lost Rothstein. He was respected by his students and he knew history. It was not easy to build a department.

When I came to Jefferson, there were no calendars of lessons for teachers to follow in providing instruction. Shortly after I came to Jefferson, I was talking to Adele Vocel, sent by the superintendent, to advise and assist Barbara Ford. She was a woman who was soon to become

164

principal of Franklin Delano Roosevelt High School. Vocel was a tough lady. When a fight broke out in the hall, one student pulled a knife. She walked up to him and demanded that he hand her the knife. He did so. Vocel advised me that there would be no per session monies for teachers to help write curriculum. The job was my own.

I typed calendars of lessons in each required subject, both Global and U.S. History. Dewey had mini-courses, and putting together calendars that included all regions of the world was a challenging task. Calendars listed skill, content and concept objectives for each lesson, and outcomes of what students would have to demonstrate at the lesson's end. They would be given to teachers in each subject before the term began. Next came homework assignment sheets. I constructed them and asked teachers to assist in noting pages in each text which a student should read each night before answering specific questions. Each homework assignment required students to use dictionaries or text glossaries in defining essential words, to answer content related questions, and to draw conclusions about what they had read. Improving student reading comprehension was an essential focus of instruction. Later, teachers of electives were asked to develop their own calendars and homework assignment sheets in courses they would teach.

Building a department was slow. I was looking for teachers who were knowledgeable, determined, creative, and would have high expectations regarding what their students could do. I created a very fine department. Ed Seidlinger, who would be the most important teacher in developing courses in criminal justice and business law, was a little rough around the edges. His speech pattern was pure Brooklyn/ Queens, but he had always wanted to be a lawyer and he would work very hard. He loved his kids and they loved him. Carol Polcovar, a woman in her 50's, was a hippy type concerned with human and women's rights. I asked her to develop a course in civil law, including issues she believed important, and she created a really nice elective course. Students learned how to initiate civil cases against individuals who brought them harm. Lynette and Michael Alexander, two younger African Americans were wonderful. They planned and taught methodically, and were loved by their students. Both would later become administrators. Lynette came to teach an introduction to law, and I would ask her to open Sealy Assembly programs because she was so personable, well dressed and well spoken. Martin Buchman was a soft spoken creative teacher whom I asked to introduce Advanced Placement American History and he did so.

Students knew he was serious and so were they. One of the most amazing examples of what a teacher could do, involved a young man whose first name was Mike (and whose last name I have forgotten). He was a tall thin fellow of Irish descent, a graduate of Columbia University. He spoke the most beautiful, sophisticated English. When one came to his class, not only did they witness serious, high level instruction and learning, but one could observe his students speaking the most wonderful, sophisticated English. They followed the lead of their teacher. He inspired his students and was a real role model. The idea that the color of the teacher is the most important factor relating to the seriousness of learning is nonsense.

Many students at Jefferson had to repeat subjects, and given my background at Dewey as Independent Study coordinator, I introduced an independent study program at

Jefferson. Instead of a fifth class, I recruited Pat Walz, a wonderful, soft spoken lady who came in each day from Staten Island, to become the independent study coordinator. Each day, during two consecutive student lunch periods, Pat would meet with about five students each period who would make up work in required courses. Students could take courses which they did not pass, not being offered in class during the current term. She would give each a homework assignment sheet, require students to complete one or two lessons and return the following week during that student's assigned day. They would show their work and discuss its content. A student who completed a unit and passed an examination at the end of the term received credit for the course. For a time, I created a resource center adjacent to my office, where students could find textbooks, law related magazines and two computers, which we were only beginning to use. John Dewey had classrooms built around resource centers, and if properly run, they had great value. A para-professional operated the center during the three student lunch periods at Jefferson. She distributed materials and made certain that students returned them. Teachers assigned projects from supplementary readings which were placed on reserve in the resource center. Law magazines, contributed by our Mentor law firm of Robinson and Silverman were located in a special section. A project sheet directed students to read and answer specific questions about articles related to criminal and civil cases. The resource center also gave students a quiet place during their lunch hours, something many might not have had at home. A computer, connected to NYCENET, an early NYC Board of Education website, and one on which a student could also do word processing was placed in the resource center. Carol Beck, removed the paraprofessional during the three periods that she was working in the social studies resource center. With no one there to supervise students, and make certain that students returned materials, the resource center had to close.

A good supervisor must figure out how best to place his people. I asked Guy Fraser to teach economics. He was an older man of West Indian Background. He was good at it and in moving students to understand the importance of economics in their own lives. Michael Braddock, a teacher who lived in the community and supervised the night center, was very well respected. He knew a little less history than I would have liked, but he worked very hard. I asked Mike to teach civil service examination preparation, part of the law program and he did so with enthusiasm. He did a wonderful job. On one occasion, Mike and I spoke at a UFT conference about what it takes to be an effective teacher in a   difficult learning environment. One teacher, whom I had to get rid of, was a tall, energetic looking African American male teacher. Still a regular substitute, I was certain that he would do well. His lesson plans were methodical and he knew the dynamics of a lesson. One problem was that he didn't like our children. One day, I found that he would not admit a student to his class. I knocked on his door and told him that he could not refuse to admit a student. He gave me an argument. Looking at his grading indicated a more serious problem. Only 25% of the students in his classes received passing grades. When I called him into the office to speak with him, he insisted he was right because "he had higher standards." In my opinion, he was a monster. At the end of the term, I prevailed upon the principal to release him. He was later appointed on his regular license to South Shore High School where friends told me that he continued similar practices.

The law institute I was asked to create, shortly after Coppin became superintendent, required a great deal of planning. There was hardly a student at Jefferson whose life was not affected in some way by those involved in enforcing the law. East New York remains a high crime area. There is a great deal of poverty. Single mothers are very common and dependence upon government for economic survival remains high. In meeting with Barbara Ford and others I asked whether there was a person involved with the law after whom we might name our institute. I was told that Lloyd G. Sealy had been the first black police commander in Brooklyn South, and that he had passed away only a short time before. Thus, the Lloyd G. Sealy Institute for Law and Government Services was created.

The person I asked to develop the first course, a course in criminal law, was Ed Seidlinger. He, I and Richard Lehrer, a guidance counselor who had earned his law degree at night, developed a curriculum for the six-month course. We reviewed and purchased law related books, and I contacted the Citywide Law Mentor program and looked for opportunities to draw upon its resources. Students learned about legal procedures, and the types of crimes for which one could be prosecuted under state and federal laws. He visited criminal courts and Lehrer helped enrich lessons by sharing his legal experiences.

Carol Polcovar's Civil Law class focused on how individuals could protect their rights and interests against both other individuals and government. Issues related to family law were meaningful for students.

A third course which was introduced and which I taught was Constitutional Law. I loved the subject involved. Beginning with the study of the constitution and the development of judicial review in the decisions of John Marshall, the course focused on case law relating primarily to first and fourteenth amendment cases. Cases involving freedom of religion, the extent of free speech, in times of peace and war, and freedom of assembly, the right to privacy and fourteenth amendment cases related to civil rights were included. Students assumed roles as plaintiffs and defendants, learned how to present moral and constitutional arguments and analyzed Supreme Court decisions. Coppin observed my constitutional law class before granting me tenure as an assistant principal. Before discussing Supreme Court decisions related to first amendment cases dealing with religion, it was important to consider why religion was such an emotional subject. The lesson was motivated by discussing the issues involved in the Scopes Trial, and it was enriched by students viewing parts of the film, *Inherit the Wind.* After viewing the first frames of the video, students were asked why townspeople greeted William Jennings Bryan, who came to prosecute John Scopes (the biology teacher who taught about the theory of evolution in violation of the law) with such enthusiasm. Students explained that life is difficult and that religion and the idea of salvation and an afterlife are important to them. Viewing the second part of the film, students identified the strongest argument given by Clarence Darrow in defending Scopes, that human reason is our greatest gift and must be exercised in a way that permits scientific expression. It concluded with students debating whose arguments were stronger and in seeking an answer to the question of why religion is such an emotional issue. Every student was involved in the lesson.

Of greatest benefit to the Sealy Institute program was our getting a Mentor Law firm to work with our students through the citywide run Mentor Program. Robinson Silverman was amazing. Trips were arranged by the firm for our students to visit Federal Appeals Court in New York and listen to the decisions of the justices on cases dealing with constitutional law. Having briefed cases in my class, students understood fully what was taking place. The firm hired twenty of our students to work during the summer. Its attorneys came to Jefferson and worked with our students in preparing them to compete in a city-wide law competition. Its issues of law related magazines were placed in the resource center, and worksheets directed students to projects based upon readings in those magazines. Robinson Silverman provided funding for a law and social science journal at Jefferson called *The Examiner*.

Remembering the excellent publication at Jefferson called the *Liberty Bell* when I was a student, I was going to call our law journal by that name. The principal objected since such a publication was supposed to be produced by the English department; it had not been produced in years. Robinson-Silverman's commitment to Jefferson was amazing, it is indicative of the kinds of relationships with the world of business that should be developed in all high schools.

Realizing what was possible through such contacts, I developed especially close relations with police, corrections, fire, and sanitation departments and with the taxi and limousine commission. This was especially important after we introduced civil service preparation courses. Their speakers came to our classes and discussed not only issues but offered insights into how students could become police officers or fire fighters. Students visited the police academy and the fire training facilities on Randall's island. Members of these departments came as honored guests to the Lloyd G. Sealy Institute graduation ceremonies each year. Our most honored guest and speaker each year was Mrs. Sealy, until her untimely death.

It is interesting that when I first came to Jefferson virtually any student work hung on a hall bulletin board was destroyed. Each time something was torn down, students in the Institute helped me to replace it. After a few years, almost all bulletin boards in the halls on the second floor contained student work, and nothing was desecrated.

In my third year at Jefferson, I was given tenure. The usual period could have been up to five years, but I believe that the superintendent had the ability to shorten that period. As required, I submitted a packet containing calendars of lessons, homework assignment sheets, departmental directives and accounts of staff development. Seeing the work I was doing, Coppin asked me to assume the position of lead assistant principal in social studies for the Brooklyn High School Superintendency. There were many large high schools in the Brooklyn high school superintendency (Jefferson, Tilden, Bushwick, Wingate, Erasmus, Sheepshead Bay, Murrow, Madison, Dewey, Franklin D. Roosevelt, and New Utrecht...). Each had a social studies department chairperson. My position as lead AP was to plan and conduct monthly meetings. It involved reading about all initiatives, state and district wide, and sharing them with all of the assistant principals in charge of social studies. I invited vendors from publishing companies, anxious to display textbooks and support materials. They were pleased when called and asked to sponsor lunches. Speakers were invited. Each meeting was programmed to take place in a different high school where assistant principals could discuss programs unique to their school which could be incorporated into other schools.

On February 26, 1992, I was present only minutes after two students were shot to death on the second floor, not more than 50 yards from my office. It was a day that Mayor David Dinkins had planned to visit the school. One student was dead on the spot. The second was still breathing but died shortly thereafter. Both had been shot in the head.

In a *New York Times* article (February 27, 1992) entitled, *Where a Youth Program Maintains a Burial Fund,* N.R. Kleinfeld described what police believed was the causation of the killings.

"In the gritty, insular world of East New York, adolescent life can end over a book bag, a snide remark or a betrayal.... Detectives said they had not yet pulled together the pieces, but said that a long festering feud led Khalil Sumpter, 15 years old, to walk up to Ian Moore, 17 and his friend Tyrone Sinkler, 16, and shoot them dead in the hallway of Thomas Jefferson High School in Brooklyn. ...Mr. Sumpter and Mr. Sinkler had been arrested in a robbery case. Although Mr. Sinkler went to jail of the crime, Mr. Sumpter did not. Sinkler thought Sumpter gave him up in the robbery."

That was the basis of a feud resulting in death.

Joyce Coppin immediately came to the school. Students were ushered into the auditorium. Coppin and I joined in leading students in reciting the twenty third psalm (The Lord is my Shepherd....) Moving to lift the spirits of people in my department, I went to the cafeteria and had a cart filled with cups of coffee. I remember sharing with them my feeling that as teachers in Jefferson, we were doing God's work.

For the next few days, the tone at Jefferson was one of quiet. Students understood what had happened. I felt that perhaps there was a new beginning. It was not to be. Carol Beck issued directives that each afternoon, students in all classes were to be brought to the auditorium to hear a flood of speakers. Each day saw another black "community leader" including Sonny Carson, Al Sharpton and later Jesse Jackson come to address students. The best speaker was Jackson. He implored students not to resort to violence and to make positive decisions to improve their lives. When the bell rang at 2:20 P.M. even though he was in the middle of his speech, most of the students left. Speaker after speaker, day after day, had left most students weary. The worst speaker, in my opinion, was Carl McCall, who would later become New York State Comptroller. McCall told students that "this is what white people wanted." I don't know if he really believed what he said or if it just simply came out of his mouth, but it was said. Knowing how many of the teachers in my department cared, half of whom were white, standing in the auditorium at this moment, I felt sick to my stomach.

Each day, for weeks, Beck brought in new "leaders." Her husband, a white man, who had taught at Lafayette High School, came in to videotape each speech.

184

He saw his wife as a heroine whose courage as a leader would later be touted, perhaps even in the movies. It was terrible. A tone of quiet seriousness was replaced by planned disruption. I was never asked to attend a cabinet meeting in which the killings were discussed. One day Beck brought an attorney, Ron Kuby, to introduce him to me. He was a left wing civil rights attorney who worked closely with William Kunstler (perhaps the most radical attorney at that time). He defended the killer. Beck later testified that fear of being a victim in the Brownsville / East New York environment was legitimate and should be a mitigating factor in explaining the killings. I do not know the outcome of the case.

Just a few weeks before the killings, I had been contacted by Adele Vocel; she encouraged me to apply for the AP social studies position at FDR High School. I was going to do so, but changed my mind just before the killings. I felt that Jefferson was indeed my school. In retrospect, Beck may have had difficulty in functioning after the killings. She repeatedly told people that she was in the process of building a dormitory in the neighborhood for her students, and that the Walt Disney Company had promised to build a domed structure for African plants across the street from the school on a vacant lot.

During the summer of 1992, I served as site supervisor of the summer school at Edward R. Murrow High School. Coppin had asked to me assume this position. This was certainly a reward. Murrow was an important and well run school. It was the school where Saul Bruckner was principal and it contained the offices of the Superintendency (Coppin's office). Most commendable about Murrow was its special education program. Students who were hearing impaired, blind or disabled in other ways were engaged in using computers, and main streamed, which allowed them to achieve academically. I remember one paralyzed student using a pencil in his mouth to log on. It was a wonderful program. With the excellent computer skills of the AP science, Ira Cohen, transportation cards were distributed to all who needed to them, and Regents examinations were carefully planned and executed. I observed a number of teachers and assisted one teacher who regularly taught only homebound students with lesson planning for a larger classroom. The summer was a success. One innovation of my own at Murrow was to have security personnel direct students without classes to the library during their free period. The halls, previously noisy, became quiet.

The following summer, Coppin directed me to organize the summer school at Thomas Jefferson. I had already spoken to people at Murrow and looked forward to being site supervisor at Murrow. Now I would be at Jefferson. My experiences that summer were terrible. The person to whom I had to turn to program students for summer school was the assistant principal in charge of guidance. That lady was recently appointed on an interim acting line, and was not assigned to summer school. She was angry and she may have blamed me. I offered her per-session (additional money provided by summer school) for her assistance. She accepted the money but never directed her counselors to program students for summer school. When I learned that the acting AP guidance had not done the programming only days before students were to report, I went to Beck. Beck simply stated that Toby could not find the time. I called Ken Weisman, who was in charge of summer schools, and got permission to retain Richard Lehrer, a guidance counselor, and together we programmed the school. This was only days before students were to report. However shaky its start, we got off the ground. After the first week of summer school, Ken Weissman, who headed the summer school program city wide, appointed the AP of special education from Jefferson as an additional supervisor. I did not really know this gentleman well. He replaced Lena Medley who had been the AP in charge of special education and who had been removed to work at Coppin's office, where she was to be groomed to be a principal. I asked this gentleman to assume one simple task, to develop the end of term Regents testing schedule. He said he would. I sent him to Weissman's Office in Manhattan to get instructions regarding rules and preparation for testing. He didn't give a damn. On the day of testing, instead of reporting by 7:00, he came to school at 10:00 A.M. He had failed to place examinations in envelopes with classroom designations. He had also failed to get the first part of the English Regents, and I had to get into my car and go to schools that had extra copies of that examination. At Jefferson that summer, I did the best I could. I organized security so that there would be someone patrolling on each floor. Rather than bar students who came late in the concrete courtyard, I asked the security personnel to admit students, who came late after being scrutinized, and send them to their classes. I included a small number of special education students in regular classes (one period they received help from a special education teacher). I also kept one higher math class alive although it had only about 10 students. The alternative was to kill the class at Jefferson, and God knows that it would have hurt some of our better students. Given the reality, I did a good job. Given the lack of support from Beck, who was about to retire, the sabotage by the future AP of guidance at Jefferson, and the incompetence of the AP special education, I thought I deserved a medal. Out of nowhere, I had been assigned to captain the Titanic and I had done the best I could. Teachers had taught, students took required tests and grades were submitted to central. Weissman thought I had spent too much money in keeping the math class. In the future, he would assign me as roving supervisor of social studies during the summer but not as a site supervisor.

One occurrence which remained with me, involved the treatment of a student by a police officer. I had always been on friendly terms with the police officer assigned to Jefferson. He was a tall, good looking black man whom I had heard telling students to conduct themselves well with their teachers, given that they chose to work at Jefferson. I respected him. One day, an English teacher asked a young lady to go across the street to get him a coffee from the bodega. Students were not permitted to leave the school. The young lady, who did so, was intelligent and not a "tough." Suddenly, I saw the police officer push her into the school in handcuffs. Outside, he is said to have thrown her against the wall and placed her in handcuffs. I asked what she had done. He told me to mind my own business. I insisted that I was the principal and that I had a right to know. We called her parents, and she was eventually released. Topping off this wonderful summer school experience at Jefferson was a bizarre occurrence involving our new principal, Lena Medley. On the last day of the summer term, I stopped two men, whom I did not know from entering the building. In marched Medley, and she asked me how dare I stop them. One man was her husband and the second a photographer who had come to take

192

pictures of her at Jefferson. Medley was to be the new principal. I began to think of finding a way out.

In the spring of 1992, Coppin sent Lena Medley, back to Jefferson. Medley had been the assistant principal in charge of special education at Jefferson until, I believe 1991. After witnessing students throwing a desk down the stairs and just missing Superintendent Coppin during one of her visits, Medley had confided to me that she hated the school. She had been taken to Coppin's office to obviously prepare for a future principalship. Politics was politics. Coppin was intent upon having a black principal at Jefferson. Now Lena was returned. After a few days, Medley called a meeting of the school staff and announced that she was now co-principal and would be the future principal. New York State law requires interviews for candidates during which they are interviewed by parents, teachers and representatives of the school administration. Selected candidates would then be interviewed and the person selected would have to win the approval of the City School's Chancellor. This did not stop Medley. At the staff meeting she called, she stated, "They came to me and said, Lena would you like to be the principal of Thomas Jefferson High School?" and I said, "Yes I would." From that day in the spring, despite Beck's presence, she walked around as if she was the principal. Interviews were later conducted for candidates. It was a show like the Moscow show trials.

In order for her appointment to appear legitimate, interviews had to be conducted. While knowing it was a joke, I agreed to be one such candidate. I wanted to have an opportunity to share my thoughts and feelings. During the interview, I was not introduced to the interviewers (most of whom I did not know) as a person who had successfully served as the assistant principal at Jefferson for eight years. The only people whom I knew in this committee were Joyce Coppin and Frieda Homer. To the seven or eight others, I was a stranger. I began by explaining that I had succeeded at Jefferson and that I had a vision for the future. I came prepared to explain the programs I had created, but had little opportunity to do so. Having placed students in jobs in our Mentor law firm, one idea I had prepared to present involved placing our students in internships in companies located in nearby industrial parks and teaching them skills. I never was given the opportunity to do so. Coppin sat back, rolled her eyes, and people whom I did not know questioned me as if I was an outsider, fully knowing who was going to be the principal. We know who was selected.

The CSA (Council of Supervisors and Administrators) contract allowed assistant principals to apply for vacancies in other high schools. I was to serve at Jefferson for one more year. In 1995, I transferred to George Westinghouse Vocational and Technical High School. I came in the last days of summer school, took copies of calendars of lessons and personal belongings and left. I knew that my decision was rational, but my guts were turning. I had hired and worked closely with virtually every person in my department. We had created programs and worked together for our kids. I felt shame in leaving people with whom I had shared experiences on a daily basis for so many years. Yet, I knew it was the right thing to do.

Chapter XI– George Westinghouse: My Vocational Experience

George Westinghouse Vocational and Technical High School is located in downtown Brooklyn. It is an architecturally unique building. The area surrounding the school contains court houses and lively restaurants. The neighborhood was a dramatic improvement over Pennsylvania Avenue in the East New York section of Brooklyn. The principal was Louis Rappaport, a well spoken professional of Jewish ethnicity and his assistants were Irish, African American and Italian. The school was an all boys vocational high school. Most of its students were either African American or Latino. Students took courses in construction design and electronics. In some ways it was tougher than Jefferson. At Westinghouse, delinquent students broke the lights in a stairwell, before

197

snatching a chain from another student, and at times committed acts of sabotage by jamming keys in the locks of classroom doors. There were also a great many positive things in the school. First, I was given $15,000 with which to purchase books for a student population of about 1500, the same as Jefferson's. At Jefferson, I received a yearly allocation of no more than $3,500 and I had to find books on my own. Rappaport met with his assistant principals regularly. Cabinet meetings focused on educational initiatives and evaluating their success, which he called a "Quality" approach. We were asked to read books about quality control in industry and to consider how its concepts could be applied in education. His people had adopted the idea that one could maintain on-going analysis and improve the quality of instruction. The school focused primarily on preparing students to obtain positions in the fields   of electronic and building construction. In the course of a school year, a model house was built in the backyard.

Supervisors at Westinghouse were professionals. One AP was Jean Claude Brizard, an African American whose family had come from the West Indies. As a physics teacher, he had moved all of his students to excel. Five years down the line, he would become the principal of Westinghouse.

Since the late 1960's and the political upheavals that followed, the idea of phasing out vocational schools in New York City became more popular. There was a call for "democratization," the idea that all students had to be prepared for college and academic careers. The oft repeated notion, picked up and popularized by the liberal media, was that encouraging African American students to attend vocational schools was somehow meant to relegate them to inferior positions in society. In reality, immigrants who in recent years came to this country as plumbers or electricians, have been able to do very well. During the recent flooding of my home after Super Storm Sandy, the electrician who restored my power came from the West Indies, as was the wonderful guy who installed a new boiler and water heater, who came from Haiti. Both are doing very well.

At Westinghouse, I was deeply impressed by the quality of shop teachers and how they taught. I developed a wonderful relationship with an electronics teacher who was of Hispanic background. He was hurt on a construction site and became a teacher. Given that he was one of the teachers whom I was asked to observe, he asked if I could help him with lesson planning. It was joyful. I explained how you formulate an evaluative aim (a question students would be require to answer demonstrating learning at the end of the lesson,) how it was important to formulate and list skill, content and concept objectives before even structuring one's lesson, how one motivates a lesson and the importance of good questioning. The next day, he showed me his lesson plan. It was meticulously typed and was covered with plastic. In the course of the lesson, he did many things which were excellent. He began by asking students to read a problem he had placed on the blackboard. He asked that they explain the steps that had to be taken in constructing an electrical circuit and they did so. Students demonstrated reading comprehension. He then told students to proceed with their work. Upon their completion, he asked students to explain what they did, and to describe the procedures they followed as was required in the evaluative aim. One could see that students had learned because they had constructed their circuits and could explain what they had achieved. This was practical education, and one could see that learning had taken place.

My office at Westinghouse was a huge room containing tables, a huge wall of book shelves, and file cabinets. It was not a separate room but a place where teachers could come, sit down and prepare their work. It was their space and I was a part of it. I cleaned out the place, something that hadn't been done in 25 years. Books, dealing with each subject were organized in the wall library for departmental use. I provided calendars of lessons to teachers, and homework sheets (newly paginated with the assistance of teachers) to students. These were modified to infuse the importance of inventions and technology and their place in history. This was logical since Westinghouse was fundamentally a school of technology. As at Jefferson, videotapes and readings for inclusion in lessons were organized. I hired Valerie Gerard, who would later become the AP social studies at Westinghouse and taught her how to conduct lessons using groups in analyzing materials and coming to conclusions. There was a very bright and knowledgeable history teacher, Allen, and I prevailed on him to teach Advanced Placement American History. An Independent Study program, which I introduced, allowed students to make up work during their lunch period (similar to the program introduced at Jefferson). A wonderful woman, Dulcie Reid became its coordinator. Students came to her religiously during assigned lunch periods, and she added short research projects using computers to her requirements. Dulcie and I worked closely together, and she and I organized a Martin Luther King, Jr. Day memorial assembly. She recruited the talent. I spoke with the deans of the New York City

Technical College which adjoined Westinghouse and they allowed us to use their auditorium. Before I left Westinghouse, I recommended her for the AP social studies position. It was probably because she was a woman in this male dominated environment that she was not seriously considered. Interestingly, years later, Valerie Girard whom I hired at Westinghouse, and would later bring to New Dorp, would return to Westinghouse as its assistant principal in charge of social studies.

In addition to supervising the social studies department, I was also asked to supervise the language department. Given the number of technical courses students were required to take, they could take only two years of a foreign language. Most took Spanish. In addition, Westinghouse had a large Hispanic population. The Spanish teacher and I agreed that many students, especially Hispanic students, could pass the three year Regents examination in Spanish if given an opportunity to do so. I went to Rappaport and he agreed to allow me to order Regents Examination in Spanish. Students were given an additional opportunity to create records of academic success in addition to their technological schooling, and students who took that Regents did well on them. My aim was to maximize student performance wherever possible.

The only person with whom I had difficulty at Westinghouse was the chapter chairman of the UFT (United Federation of Teachers). Our conflict was not over departmental policy or the preservation of teacher rights. He was a tall, good looking guy, who carried himself with an air of importance. The principal gave him a great deal of deference. My first conflict with him was my insistence that he let students who came after the late bell into his classroom. He insisted that barring them was consistent with his high standards and was an educational device. From an administrative viewpoint it was both an educational and safety issue. A student left in the hall could be hurt. He admitted students as I asked but there was no love to be lost between us. The principal wanted to avoid conflict with him, so I was advised to take it easy as well. I had established my credibility, and my relations with my teachers and other staff members were excellent.

Chapter XII – Idealism is not enough

After two years at Westinghouse, I made a terrible mistake. The Board of Education offered an incentive to encourage retirement of older teachers and   supervisors. The idea was to get "new blood" and probably a 'better" ethnic mix into the system. I had often thought that at some future time, I might seek a position with a Jewish High School. I spoke enough Hebrew to observe a class. I knew the music and history of the Jewish people and actually believed the claims in the Jewish press that there was a demand for high quality Jewish educational leaders. I felt I had all the qualifications to assume a new and exciting career. I applied for the position of Assistant Principal at the Solomon Schechter Hebrew High School located in the Jewish Theological Seminary inupper Manhattan. The Seminary trains those who would become

Conservative rabbis and cantors, both men and women.

My daughter Robin, took courses dealing with Jewish thought and mysticism at the seminary. It is a beautiful building and its library is magnificent. It has thousands of volumes that any historian, especially one with a Jewish bent would love to read. The JTS is across the street from Colombia University. I was impressed by the environment.

Meeting the woman who was the principal of the high school, I felt certain reservations, but in the contract there was an agreement that I would teach at least one course in American History and this encouraged me. I signed a contract shortly before handing in my retirement papers for the New York City Board of Education. The people in my department at Westinghouse treated me to lunch in a restaurant on Montague St. and we parted on the best of terms.

The principal of this high school was a woman whose husband was a Conservative rabbi in Connecticut. The school was given only a fixed number of rooms for its program. Coming in before school began, I got a techie teacher from Westinghouse to take viruses off the half a dozen computers available for student use, and on the first day of school, I gave each student a new blank disk so that no new viruses would be brought in to Schechter. Contacting colleagues who taught science, I purchased the best books in biology, chemistry and physics. I ordered excellent history text books. I found excellent desks in an attic in the seminary and set up another classroom. I was well prepared when students reported. The entire school had no more than 100 students. Classes were very small.

From the first, I sensed difficulty. After observing a wonderful Hebrew teacher and writing a constructive observation report, which the teacher appreciated, I was told by the principal that I could use only her check list to evaluate a lesson. My best skills were in teacher training, and an opportunity to improve instruction was denied. I had constructed a wonderful bulletin board containing posters, graphics and maps revealing important events in Jewish History which I had saved over many years. I put it up outside our main office and I saw this as something which would advertise our mission there for the entire year. After two weeks it was removed and replaced by a handful or student papers with chicken scratched math problems. I was supposed to teach a history class, as indicated in my contract, and she gave the class to a 22 year old young man who was taking classes at Columbia University (across the street) and whose family she may have known. I offered to infuse the Jewish Historical experience into both world and American History curricula and this was denied. The

210

principal explained to me one day how she would dress as a witch on Halloween. My own children had gone to a Conservative Hebrew Day school in Brooklyn and the celebration of Halloween was discouraged. Since when did Jewish educators celebrate a holiday that preceded All Saints Day?

Student files indicated that many of the students had far from stellar academic records and were going to this school as an alternative to public school. One day, she gave me an argument for not picking up jock straps students had left in the hallway. I was becoming sick to my stomach. I had left a position in which I excelled and was respected for a world of make believe.

In mid year, I resigned from my position. During the remainder of the year, I worked as a consultant for per-session pay in a Junior High School in Manhattan, and later was given a position by Superintendent Coppin as an assistant to a very confused principal at Bushwick High School in Brooklyn. I was asked by Coppin to assist the principal by observing lessons and working with teachers since the principal was supposedly overwhelmed by redesign. Having been a "failing school" in terms of student success, the school was being restructured so that new programs could be introduced and teachers who wanted out would be given the opportunity to seek positions in other schools. The principal never let me do what Coppin had asked me to do. A Latino, evidently proud of this, he walked the halls conversing in Spanish. His school day was filled with meetings with communal groups, mostly Spanish speaking. During one observation we did jointly, he gave an excellent evaluation report to a bi-lingual teacher whose entire lesson was in Spanish (it was supposed to be in both English and Spanish).

I asked Coppin whether there were any AP vacancies in the district. She sent me to a mini-school that was part of re-design at Erasmus Hall High School. Other than observing disorder and seeing children with their heads on their desks, I saw little of value in this school. The principal of this school also wanted to see me out of the door as soon as possible. She stressed that her entire program focused on learning made possible by the right side of the brain. She asked whether I was aware of education in that way. This was nonsense.

I called Westinghouse and asked for an interview with the new principal. I was interested in returning to the world I knew best. The Assistant Principal in charge of administration, J.C. Brizard, who knew how hard I had worked at Westinghouse as an AP, urged the principal to meet with me. I met with him, explained what I had done, and asked for assistance in returning to my former position. He was in the mid-fifties as was I. He looked at me as if I was 100. He knew nothing of how I had shaped a department. He turned and said to me, "I need new blood." That was the end of that interview. I heard that a year later he died of a heart attack.

During the summer of 1998, I met a former teacher from Westinghouse, Charlie, who had become an assistant principal at New Dorp High School in Staten Island. I spoke to him about my less than satisfying retirement, and he asked if I would consider coming to New Dorp. The principal of New Dorp was Liz Sciabarra, sister of one of my favorite students at John Dewey High School, Chris

Sciabarra. We had once worked together during a summer school at Brooklyn Technical High School. I called her, went for an interview, met with her, other AP's, a union representative and most likely a parent representative. She promised to take the steps to allow me to assume the position of AP social studies at New Dorp High School and she did so. Just before the Christmas holiday in 1998, I went to the Board, rescinded my resignation and was appointed as assistant principal social studies to New Dorp High School. I would be at New Dorp for ten years.

Chapter XIII – Going Home   Again

They say that you can't go home again. Returning to a position as an assistant principal in charge of social studies in a New York City public high school, for me, was an example of going home again. Having been a roving supervisor of social studies during a number of summers, I was familiar with all boroughs except Staten Island. As a child I remember being taken to a Staten Island cemetery by my mother's cousin to visit the graves of his two brothers; they had died of tuberculosis shortly after immigrating to America. At one point in time, in the other boroughs, Staten Island was known for its farms and cemeteries.

After the opening of the Verrazano Bridge, Staten Island began to receive an infusion of people, mostly   from

216

Brooklyn. The largest single ethnic group migrating from Brooklyn was Italian, and Italian supervisors and teachers were more evident in this borough than in any other. Most of the teachers at New Dorp came from either Staten Island or New Jersey. The high tolls on the Verrazano Bridge discouraged travel from Brooklyn into Staten Island. By the time I left New Dorp, the toll I paid to cross the bridge from Brooklyn to Staten Island was $13.50. By agreement with the state, Staten Islanders paid less when leaving and returning, but tolls dissuaded many who would have assured a more representative ethnic mix. Staten Island remains different from the other four boroughs in the City of New York. It is really a kind of suburb. It is a wonderful borough. Most students live in low one or two family homes and would be considered middle class. Some, mostly minority kids, travelled from the eastern end of the island with the Highland Avenue bus from the less affluent projects. Staten Island is the home to large numbers of policeman, firemen and others who work for government. Given that a ferry crossed from Staten Island to Wall Street, many of its people also worked in that location. On the 11th of September, 2001, when the World Trade Center was attacked and thousands died, among its dead were 14 New Dorp High School graduates, many of its residents were among the more than 300 firemen who perished. Many of those who lost their lives were the parents of our children.

The school was a well integrated and racially mixed school. There were Italians, Irish, Latino, Jewish, African Americans and many Albanians. A nearby high school for science, where only Russian was taught, drained off many of the students who would have been part of the top tier at New Dorp, as did a nearby successful Catholic High

School. New Dorp High School, off Hylan Boulevard was located on New Dorp Lane. New Dorp High School is found in a large three story building, able to hold over 2,300 students. It has a suburban style football field, grand stands, a baseball field and tennis courts.

When I reported to New Dorp, my reception was mixed. Cathy Piszco, a good teacher, had been the acting-interim chairperson and resented being displaced. At New Dorp, I would build a fine department. I saw my role primarily as a teacher trainer. My experiences prior coming to New Dorp served me well.

Liz Sciabarra, the principal who hired me, was a very intelligent and dynamic woman. By the end of the school year, she was recruited by the Board of Education to be in charge of creating schools for the gifted throughout the city. The person selected as the new principal was Deirdre DeAngelis. DeAngelis, a woman in her early thirties, had been the Assistant Principal in charge of special education at John Dewey High School. She was a tall blond, athletic woman with a great deal of energy and was an ardent sports fan. She had met her future husband in Staten Island's Yankee Stadium and she would be married by a justice of the peace in that stadium a few years later. She was admittedly not an intellectual, but she was smart, hard working and was fundamentally honest. When she needed to do something which she felt I might consider undesirable, I could see it in her face. She would often share personal history and was more open in that respect than any previous supervisor I had ever known. Although I didn't recall it, she said that she had been a student at Dewey and had been in my class. She had gone on and later returned to Dewey as a teacher, and then became AP in charge of special education. Her being Italian and a woman were probably factors in her appointment to New Dorp. She was highly energetic and had a very good survival instinct. In the "Age of Bloomberg" it would lead her to break up her own school into six mini schools, a form of redesign, while remaining at the helm.

At New Dorp, the assistant principals in charge of English, Science, Foreign Languages, Special Education, Guidance, Business and Administration were women. Math, Physical Education and Social Studies had male AP's.

When I assumed full command of the department in February 1998, I worked closely with a secretary who typed calendars of lessons for the department. As the term progressed, homework assignment sheets, paginated (pages for students to read for each lesson) for the textbooks at New Dorp, were reproduced and provided for students in each required subject class. A file of readings, which could be used in teaching each lesson in each subject was established. The readings contained charts and graphs, materials which could enrich lessons. Videotapes were purchased in each subject area and these were placed in file cabinets in chronological order in the department office. Whenever I went to a luncheon for AP's of social studies, during which publishers presented their books, volumes of documents and supportive readings would be acquired and placed in the office. Teachers knew where to come to obtain materials and did so freely. Every department meeting had a professional topic, and my focus was on the importance of reading comprehension in each lesson.

One of most interesting wars I enjoyed at New Dorp was with Carolyn Gannon, Assistant Principal in charge of

Guidance. In that position, she was in charge of guidance counselors who programmed students. My personal belief was that students who demonstrated interest in history should be encouraged to take advanced placement courses in European and American History. I recall my own inability to have taken more challenging courses in this subject because my grades in math were poor. When speaking to students who had such deep interest, I would go to Gannon and ask that they be programmed for advanced placement courses. She often gave me a difficult time, but I usually won out. I did not see any malice in her position, and on some occasions, when she would extend a big hug over some triumph, it was appreciated.

During my first full term at New Dorp, I was asked to create a special program. The Gilder Lehrman Institute for American History promised New Dorp approximately $10,000 a year for materials and trips, if we would develop a program to enrich the study of American History. We recruited students and created an institute with a special program. By the end of my first year, parallel electives in American Colonial History, Civil War, American Social History, Law and Justice and Constitutional Law were introduced in the Institute. Students in this program were also programmed for Advanced Placement American History in their junior year. Trips were planned in each elective subject. I taught American Colonial History and took students to the location where Benjamin Franklin met General Howe in an attempt to prevent the continuation of the American Revolution. We visited Valley Forge (where Washington's troops had a difficult winter during the American Revolution) and Independence Hall in Philadelphia where the Declaration of Independence was written. Jeff Benjamin, who creatively taught the course about the Civil War, planned and took students on wonderful trips to Gettysburg and later to Washington, D.C. Nanci Richards, who taught American social history, took students to the Apollo Theatre in Harlem, to the Tenement museum and Chinatown on the historic Lower East Side of Manhattan.

Given my experience in obtaining a mentor law firm, we obtained support from a local firm on Staten Island, and its attorneys enriched our course in Criminal Justice. The key was getting the right people to teach each of these courses and we did so.

It takes years to build a fine department of more than 20 people. Before asking Deirdre DeAngelis to hire a teacher, I would hold interviews. I would ask teachers about courses they had taken, and how they might teach a particular lesson. I would ask what they wanted students to learn, how they might motivate the lesson, what questions they might ask to develop and what readings they might employ. I would test their knowledge base in American and world history and ask how one might teach about different crises around the world.

I would look for teachers who were knowledgeable, confident, but also willing to learn. My own basic conservatism would play a role, but not necessarily a decisive one. One of the subjects I would broach would be asking how one might teach about the Arab-Israel conflict. Admittedly, I would not hire a teacher who was radical left and would declare that the solution to the Arab-Israeli struggle was to destroy the State of Israel. One young applicant stated that a solution to the Arab Israeli conflict would require compromise that would allow all people live and develop their societies. I hired Agron Velija, a very bright young man, who was a Muslim of Albanian extraction and had a degree from a university in Bulgaria. He was a wonderful teacher whose every word inspired kids. Upon his directions, students worked in groups, and tested each other over material that would be on the following day's examination. Agron developed excellent programming skills and later became an assistant principal in charge of administration at a nearby vocational school.

One teacher sent to me by DeAngelis was Dina Episcopia (her married name was Zoleo). Dina Zoleo was one of the finest teachers I had ever met. Regarding the ability to deliver quality instruction, I considered myself to be close to the very top. In some ways she succeeded even better than her mentor. She was a beautiful young lady. Like me, Dina was clearly hyperactive. She taught at a wonderfully rapid pace. Accepting my advice regarding fine points in lesson planning and instruction, her instruction was methodical and excellent. Virtually every student participated in each lesson, and learning was evident. Noting her willingness to master required scholarship, I asked Dina to teach Advanced Placement European History which we included in the 10th grade curriculum as a higher level alternative to the normal 10th grade global studies curriculum. The funding was found to get every teacher in our department an overhead projector. It may seem funny but this was high tech before the infusion of computers. This allowed teachers to project readings and graphics on a screen in front of the room. Teachers were encouraged to reproduce maps, charts and other materials on plastic sheets using a photocopy machine. Before long, however, that technology was to be as antiquated as the bronze spear. During one department meeting, I demonstrated how one could use the internet in the classroom. I showed teachers how I had logged in,

228

accessed Michelangelo's paintings on the ceiling of the Sistine Chapel and used a projector I had purchased with Gilder Lehrman money to project it on to a screen. Before long, most teachers in my department would surpass me with ease in the use of new technologies. Dina was one of these people. While at New Dorp, I completed and published a book I had been working on, *"How to become an effective social studies teacher."* I dedicated it to Bob Shain and Dave Pinelis. Copies were given to members of the department and to all new teachers.

Nanci Richards came from Lafayette High School. Considered a less than productive school, Lafayette was broken up into mini-schools and many teachers were excessed. Nanci was a professional stand up comedian when not teaching. Her causes were civil and women's rights. My own political positions generally were center to right of center. She was somewhat left. However, she was alive, and my feeling was that she would interest and involve students in thinking seriously about the important social issues of our time. Every once in while she would show a film which I thought was a little too racy and I would tell her so. She would sort of wave me off. In hiring Nanci, our program found a teacher for an elective in American Social History. Nanci would later serve as mentor to our student teacher, Toni Ann Rugiero, whom she advised me to hire. Toni Ann knew her subject matter well, was highly energetic, and was a technology whiz kid. I would love to observe how she used a white board (where students could make additions to notes posted in lieu of using a blackboard) and other devices to engage students. I asked Toni Ann to teach Advanced Placement American History and she did so wonderfully.

Pat Hopkins and Brian Murphy were two wonderful very fine teachers. Pat was a psychology major and had a wonderful ease in teaching his students. He was later asked to serve as a dean, thus limiting his departmental teaching, but he did eventually get to teach a course in psychology. Both Pat and Brian were big guys and Murphy too would be tapped to become a dean. Murphy also had a wonderful personality and could make students feel at home. After including law within our program, Brian taught Criminal Justice.

A teacher who was greatly appreciated was Jeff Benjamin. Not only did he have a wonderful personality, but he was a Civil War buff. I do not believe there could have been a better choice for a teacher of that subject. In his class, students would feel as if they were present in each of the battles and personal struggles of those whose lives were touched during that tragic national conflict. For each year in which I served as AP social studies at New Dorp, Jeff took one or two bus loads of students to Gettysburg. Students walked where Picket's men had fallen in their failing charge, and then walked among the head stones on Cemetery Ridge. Visits were timed for November 14 when Abraham Lincoln delivered his famous Gettysburg Address and when Lincoln re-enactors would deliver the Gettysburg Address at Gettysburg. Students in his classes wrote excellent research papers about subjects related to the Civil War and entered them in the yearly Gilder Lehrman research paper competition. A number of our students won recognition for their work.

One gentleman, Anthony Cassella, a very nice man in his mid-forties had come from a junior high. In applying for the position at New Dorp, he explained that he had supervised an after school reading program. At one point, New Dorp was considering such a program and I saw him as a potential teacher for that program. He loved films and carefully planned ways in which one could teach concepts through film. I encouraged him. Using the film Casablanca, he showed how when the Germans began to sing their songs, Frenchmen in unison began to passionately sing the Marseilles. He asked why they acted as they did. Students explained they had been moved by nationalism. He took some of my tips regarding methodology and I appreciated his intelligence and commitment. Anthony was also a professional musician, and in the absence of a music teacher, DeAngelis soon asked him to work with students in providing musical ensembles on specific occasions.

One of the joys in my position as assistant principal in charge of social studies was in holding pre-observation conferences with each of my teachers. Such conferences were even more important than the post observation conferences. These conferences offered me an opportunity to discuss historical content, and methodologies which could be employed in each lesson. I pushed for the inclusion of readings and we discussed the questioning which could contribute to improving reading comprehension. In being a roving supervisor during many summers, I noticed that a terribly accepted practice involved the poor use of distributed readings. Teachers would give out a complex reading, tell Johnny to read and go on and ask Rebecca to read. Teachers would not ask the kinds of questions that would require students to demonstrate that they understood what they had read. The improvement of reading comprehension is not the task of the English department alone. As stated earlier, shop teachers at Westinghouse had made reading comprehension a must in their lessons. Questioning, when using a reading, is an art form. A teacher might begin by asking students whether there were any words one did not understand. A series of questions was then required: What is the reading about? What is its main idea? What facts are given to support that idea? Whom do you believe wrote it? Where? When? and Why? One could then ask students whether they agreed with an opinion that could be found in the reading. Reading without reading comprehension is meaningless. Literacy should be a primary function of instruction in each subject.

During our post-observation conference, I would ask teachers what students had learned and how this had been demonstrated. This should be the most important factor in deciding the quality of a teacher. Was appropriate learning evident? When necessary, we would talk about ways in which the lesson might have been improved. We were professionals working together. The only time I would ever come down on a teacher was if I saw a teacher was mean, or unprepared and faking it.

There were many more good teachers in my department at New Dorp. All of those whom I hired liked children and believed that what they were doing was important. Teachers in my department at New Dorp respected each other, and knew they could count on each other. I felt as if I was there for them. For a school to succeed, its people must be carefully selected for what they are and for what they know, and they must be given the ongoing support of supervisors who have clear ideas as to what needs to be achieved.

Chapter XIV – The Bloomberg   Revolution

September 11, 2001 was the seemingly most unreal and tragic day during my years as an educator. A plot by Arab Muslim terrorists resulted in the seizure of American passenger planes; planes filled with innocent travelers, and intentionally smashed into two of the beautiful buildings of the World Trade Center. As supervisor of the culinary arts program at New Dorp (a little addition given to me since there was no supervisor for that program) I attended a ceremony at the World Trade Center during which a number of our children were given scholarships. I had never been in those buildings before and I was amazed at the panorama of the city one could see from the tops of those buildings. Approximately 3,000 people died in the World trade center on that day. Many of those who died were firemen who went into those buildings to save people before the buildings collapsed. Fourteen of those who perished were graduates of New Dorp High School. My wife, Judy, who worked in downtown Brooklyn, shared with me her pain as she personally witnessed the planes crashing into the World Trade Center buildings and people jumping to their deaths from its top floors.

When I received the news that morning, I entered many of the social studies classes and explained as calmly as I could the tragedy that had occurred. Not knowing whether any acts of terror would follow on the ground, students were all brought down to the gymnasium in the basement. The Verrazano bridge was closed until near evening on that day, and strict searches were made of every vehicle entering the city.

Later in the day, the principal asked me to write a brief statement of explanation which could be read to students on the following day. Whatever I wrote was "cleansed." Part of my explanation was that Muslim extremists had acted to bring harm to our society and that we, as Americans would recover and bring to justice those who had taken the lives of so many of our innocent people. The word Muslim was taken out, because it was considered discriminatory. This would seem absurd, except that on that same day President Bush, in addressing the nation, also declared that Islam was really a religion of peace that had been hijacked by few extremists. Since then, we have learned there are quite a few of those "bad guys."

For weeks after the collapse of the buildings in the World Trade Center, I could smell the foul air. It was the smell of human protein or human flesh that filled the air.

Each year on the date of 9/11 that I remained at New Dorp, I took the microphone, asked students to stand in their classes and read the names of the fourteen New Dorp students who perished during that attack.

In January 2002, Michael Bloomberg became the Mayor of the City of New York. Among the first priorities on his agenda was asking the New York State legislature to give the mayor complete responsibility for running the educational system in the City of New York. The media spoke of him wanting to be the education mayor. He moved the headquarters from 110 Livingston Street in Brooklyn to the Tweed building in Manhattan, only a short distance from City Hall. Bloomberg was a self-made multimillionaire who originally won election as a Republican. As a very successful businessman, he believed the old system of top down dictates had failed as had instruction in the classroom. Bloomberg became a supporter of charter schools, privately run schools funded with public money, which were not unionized. These schools would supposedly lead to competition which would improve the quality of the product, education. Implicit was also the idea of weakening the UFT. Bloomberg appointed Joel Klein, a former Federal prosecutor to be his chancellor. Bloomberg and Klein announced that failing schools would be closed. Numerous high schools were then closed, broken up into mini-schools and reopened on the same premises. Schools and teachers in schools that performed above a norm, were to be given a monetary incentive. On paper it sounded good.

One day, it was announced that Chancellor Klein would visit New Dorp. Deirdre asked me to provide a class in which he would conduct a lesson. A wonderful social history class was selected. Klein was an attorney and we had expectations of a law related lesson or a social commentary. Klein had no idea of how to teach. He spoke a little about education and rambled from one subject to another. Deirdre might well have seen this visit as the handwriting on the wall, an act preceding a central announcement that New Dorp would be divided into mini-schools.

Neither Bloomberg, nor Chancellor Klein, ever announced details of what their overall plan for reforming the educational system in the city was. Other than the destruction of the old "failing system" there was never any announcement of any step by step approach for improving the system. I believe that the steps taken were intentionally piecemeal; their purpose was probably to avoid the opposition from previously entrenched groups. It is probably a way in which a corporate executive takes over and dismembers an adversary after a hostile takeover.

Some of its elements, meant to destroy the old system, made no sense to someone who was part of the system. The Staten Island Superintendant whom I had known disappeared from the scene and was said to have obtained a position in Queens. The Tweed building was seemingly made a center for modeling educational practices. I remember visiting Tweed one day, and seeing a number of classes that were in operation. I originally thought that they were classes meant to serve as models for new modes of instruction. A teacher told me that his class was only there for two weeks. It was a show.

Directives came by e-mail each day to principals from Tweed. In the past, AP's in charge of social studies in our high school superintendency, like assistant principals in each subject area, met to discuss professional topics. Meetings now were conducted for assistant principals in charge of social studies by a math chairman. Assistant principals in charge of English in junior high schools were included in this group. It made no sense. At first, I offered to serve as a lead AP in social studies, but I soon understood that such a group no longer really existed. We had to go to pieces of paper on a wall and write our answers to questions about elementary problems in education. Soon the Central Board hired a group of Australian educators to teach us how to teach reading. It was said that they had developed a program in Australia, which was the beginning and end all of how to teach reading. One woman began to read as one reads to a child. It was a world of make believe. This costly boondoggle made no sense whatsoever.

New mini-high schools had a principal each, and an assistant principal in charge of administration. Such schools no longer had assistant principals in charge of instruction in their respective disciplines. Principals appointed to these new schools were inexperienced graduates from a principal's academy that Klein and Mayor Bloomberg created. Where were these new schools to get experienced people to advise and people to train teachers? Do not fear! The smell of big money, millions, led to the creation of 'think tanks" that the Central Board of Education now contracted to advise principals and improve instruction. Former principals were to be advisors to new principals, while others would be hired to do teacher training. Where did they come from? They were retired principals with a sprinkling of college professors.

After retiring, I unfortunately became personally familiar with one of these think tanks for a relatively short time, *New Visions*. Its advisors were retired principals and assistant principals some of whom I knew from Brooklyn. If a new system was to be created, isn't it ironic that it was to be guided by those who were judged to have failed?

I had expected to be assigned to a number of schools in which I would help to organize their resources, develop their social studies programs and help teachers to improve instruction. A gentleman with dreadlocks of about thirty years of age was assigned as my supervisor. This handsome African American in charge of social studies was not a social studies person. He knew nothing about the subject. One day he called me in to tell me that I would be part of a team headed by a team leader whom he said was a social studies person. The team's leader turned out to be a

23 year old woman, who had been a substitute teacher for a year, in a suburban Westchester school. She told me that in any meeting, only she could speak for the group. When I offered advice to a teacher in a school in Harlem which we visited, I was given a dressing down. I attempted to model lessons at Bushwick High School and work with new teachers, only to find that when I came on Friday, each was intentionally giving an examination. A female teacher who came from the West Indies and knew virtually nothing about world history (the subject she was teaching at Jefferson) decided to be absent each Tuesday when she knew that I was coming. So much for my post-retirement experiences for *New Visions*! I had originally been asked to work for *New Visions* by an officer of the think tank who visited New Dorp and who knew that I would be retiring. *New Visions* had been contracted to help restructure New Dorp when it was decided that it would be divided into

mini-schools. The public knows nothing of these think tanks. I have never seen one article by a media expert on the subject of education about these organizations. I wonder how much *New Visions*, with its former old school principals, was paid each year by the Board of Education of the City of New York for its work in creating a new and better system.

Chapter XV– Upheaval at New   Dorp

In 2005, New Dorp was a large academic school with a population of a little over 2,300. Given its largely blue collar student population, I believed that it should have been judged moderately successful. Given my very good department, students did well on Global and American History Regents examinations. When Bloomberg Education officials began to assess comparative school performance, to determine whether their teachers and supervisors should be given merit pay, students scored 105% on the American History Regents at New Dorp. The poorest comparative results came from the English department. This should have been a primary concern and a subject of serious discussion between the principal and the English assistant principal. Focusing on the nature of English Regents examinations, I believe that steps had to be taken   to improve student vocabulary, reading comprehension, writing skills and test preparation. I know that these were goals in social studies from the vocabulary on every homework sheet and the methods discussed and demonstrated at social studies department meetings. Reading comprehension was a subject of discussion in each of my pre- and post-observation conferences, and improvement was achievable. I touted the Gilder Lehrman program to parents as the alternative for students who had a real interest in history and the social sciences as opposed to Math and Science. We got a mixed and wonderful collection of interested students. One day, I believe it was in 2005, Deirdre DeAngelis called a meeting of assistant principals and informed us that given the citywide moves, she planned to divide New Dorp into smaller "more personal" and "more successful learning communities." This was presented as a fact, not a subject for discussion.

She tried to make it more palatable by telling us that each assistant principal would supervise one school and would be like its principal. In retrospect, its initial planning with *New Visions* must have been on going for a long period of time prior to this day. Deirdre and her assistant principals in charge of administration and guidance must have known that it was coming. I did not. I remember pointing out to her the advantages of a large school, its flexibility in programming teachers, and the services it could provide for all of its students.

The plan involved breaking up the school into six mini schools. Each assistant principal would retain departmental responsibilities but also be responsible for the operations of a mini-school. Deirdre would appoint two coordinators as leaders in each mini-school who would develop its activities. Each coordinator, after attending

251

New Visions led workshops, a Baruch College class one day a week, would be granted an assistant principal's license. Each teacher would be assigned to a school. Programming would be centrally done. Students would be asked to choose a mini-school after being shown a "bells and whistles" Power Point presentation "to sell that school" created by the coordinators. This option would be given to all students, including those already in the Gilder Lehrman program. Each school would have its separate wing in the building, its own colors, its own book rooms, its own teachers and its own AP offices. Teachers in one school would most likely be unable to teach in the other schools. This student selection of mini-schools would bring an end to the high quality Gilder Lehrman program as we knew it.

It was my practice to assign each new teacher to teach the same subject twice before moving on to cover additional required subjects. The purpose was to provide continuity so that teachers would master each subject before moving on. Now, I would no longer have this ability; teachers were centrally assigned within mini-schools. Each school would have two coordinators. Deirdre, probably after consulting with Carolyn (AP Guidance) and JoAnn Codd (AP Administration), decided who the coordinators for each school would be and which teachers would be assigned to each school. I wanted Toni Ann Ruggiero to be the mini-school coordinator for Gilder, given her in depth knowledge of American History. Dina, who taught AP European History, along with a young woman from the language department, were made leaders of the Gilder Lehrman school, while Toni Ann, who taught AP American was made a coordinator of another school. Nell, a college education teacher, was the leader appointed by New Visions to conduct workshops for assistant principals and coordinators.

The model adopted was not the worst possible, because unlike many of the mini-school models, it retained subject supervisors despite limiting their freedom. One thing that DeAngelis failed to understand was that breaking up her school, would serve as an admission for the wider community that the school was among those that had failed. It was a step she was willing to take, because I am certain she believed that New Dorp was slated for division and that her own position would disappear if that happened.

What followed was somewhat chaotic. I was told to move thousands of books from my two book rooms to book rooms a few hundred feet away. Ellen, the English AP, was not keen on moving from her beautiful office to one three hundred yards away. After finally achieving the movement into separate wings, an advertising campaign was ordered. Students were given PowerPoint presentations in the auditorium and told to select which would be the school of their choice. Their choices were Corporate (business), College Now, Future Teachers, Humanities, American and Legal Studies, Math/Science, International Studies, and Liberal arts. Gilder Lehrman, as it was before, a mix of students, was gone. Many students were attracted by the idea that Math Science alone would offer a forensics course as an elective and left Gilder. This was because the only teacher of forensics was in the science department, and was assigned to the Math/Science Institute. Logic would have allowed students taking criminal law to take forensics, but this was not so. To make it appear that New Dorp had a math science program worthy of its name, I believe that most students with above average reading scores were placed in that Institute. The high quality Gilder Lehrman program at New Dorp no longer had the mix necessary for high level instruction. Many students who had no real interest in history were placed in Gilder Lehrman. It was a reminder of what I had witnessed at Dewey, when "the powers that be" changed the feeder patterns to the school. As long as 25% of the students were above average, 50% average and 25% below, one could maintain a challenging classroom environment, when two-thirds fell below average in their reading comprehension, and required remedial instruction, the quality of instruction declined.

In the winter of 2008, I was diagnosed with prostate cancer and scheduled for a procedure. Blood clots in the lungs, afterward, and a return to the hospital took a physical and emotional toll. When I returned to New Dorp, I never felt quite the same. I returned for one more year, but in June 2008, after 48 years in the system, I applied for retirement. I felt I was unable to perform at my best.

I was fortunate to have been part of a profession which I deeply loved. I am hyper by nature and my multifaceted job as a supervisor, teacher and teacher trainer provided an outlet for my energy and creativity. For me, virtually each day provided a level of excitement that made life exciting. Beyond family, there was never anything that I enjoyed as much as being a showman in a classroom.

Before leaving New Dorp I held sessions with Dina Zoleo, Agron Velija, and others who held AP licenses, in which I made them fully aware of every resource in our department and went over questions that would be asked in a job interview. I wouldn't count anyone out. I remembered my own experience at Dewey.

Our department office had a fine library devoted to every subject about which we might teach and books containing primary source documents. There were files with readings to accompany each subject in each lesson, videotapes organized by subject, calendars of lessons and homework assignment sheets, essays from previous advanced placement examinations and an array of other useful materials. Dina became my successor at New Dorp, and Agron became the AP in charge of administration at a nearby vocational high school. At times, there is justice in the system. Anthony Casella became an assistant principal in a junior high school.

Chapter XVI – Prescription for change

A serious reader of this book will already have drawn meaningful conclusions about practices that should be discontinued, and others that deserve serious consideration for the improvement of education. I will reiterate a few of my own.

1) Mayoral responsibility can be a positive development, because someone needs to be held accountable for educational decisions in the city. The mayor should convene a brain trust, perhaps of the most successful principals (on all levels), and they should have a voice in recommending a Chancellor. This should be a futuristic ongoing practice.

2) The Chancellor, in turn, should require those who apply for positions of leadership in each school to present a plan with goals for achievement for that school. That would require both research and creativity. Each plan might well be different from the others, given the diversity of our communities and the needs of different student populations.

3) It is important to introduce a system of accountability. Elementary, Middle Schools and Senior High Schools should be placed in clusters. Children in elementary school should be proficient in the skills necessary for Middle School, and those entering Senior high school should have the skills that middle schools should have provided. If students do not have the skills required in the higher level, those below should be held accountable.

4) Serious consideration should be given to expanding vocational education. Planning with community colleges, corporations and unions should consider realistic approaches to graduating students who will be able to obtain apprenticeships and set out on a path that will lead to a good income and providing the skilled technicians required in our society.

5) The way to excite passion in each teacher is to leave room for personal creativity.

6) Being leaders, however, is not without its burden. It requires accountability for student performance. High performance should be given recognition, and incentives should make teacher self-improvement possible.

7) Student education should be more personalized. Students should be understood by those who program them, and flexible programming should take into account talents and interests. Students who excel in specific subjects should be programmed for more challenging classes in those subjects while receiving support in others. Education should excite and motivate students. (This is a complex but essential element in the long term improvement of our system.).

8) The UFT has helped teachers gain decent incomes, medical benefits and retirement pensions. It has protected good people from mistreatment by narcissistic supervisors. However, it should not be paralyzed into inaction in defense of a less than

262

productive status quo. It should be a think tank for the improvement of education. It should call upon its best people and commit itself to experimentation and positive change.

9) The politics of race and nepotism need to end. The reintroduction of written examinations and model teaching requirements for those who would wish to apply for supervisory positions should be reintroduced. People who would prove themselves in this way would be eligible for appointments.

My experiences "in the trenches," have given meaning and joy to my life. It is my hope that my insights will contribute to creating a system in which each school will provide an effective and futuristic education to all of its children